# ENDEAVOUR

### A PHOTOGRAPHIC JOURNEY

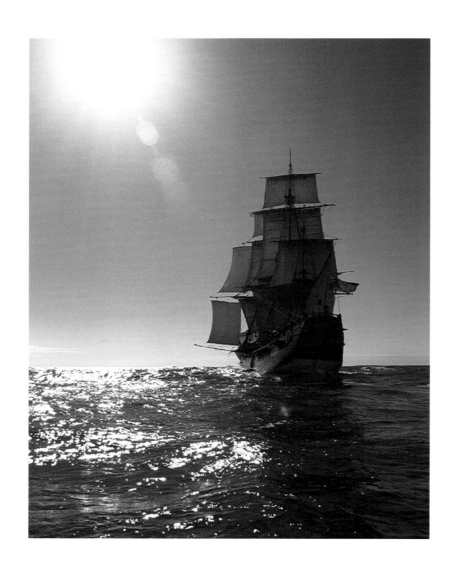

# ENDEAVOUR

## A PHOTOGRAPHIC JOURNEY

### RICHARD POLDEN

**FREMANTLE ARTS CENTRE PRESS**

in association with

**Sunday Times**

First published 1998 by
FREMANTLE ARTS CENTRE PRESS
193 South Terrace (PO Box 320), South Fremantle
Western Australia 6162
www.facp.iinet.net.au
In association with
*SUNDAY TIMES*, Perth.

Designer John Douglass.
Production Editor and Coordinator Cate Sutherland.

Typeset by Fremantle Arts Centre Press
and Printed by Sands Print Group.
Pre-Press by Complete Imaging Centre.

National Library of Australia
Cataloguing-in-publication data

Polden, Richard 1971- .
The Endeavour.

ISBN 1 86368 227 9.

1. Cook, James, 1728-1779 - Journeys - Pictorial works. 2.
Endeavour (Ship: Replica) - Pictorial works. 3. Australia
- Discovery and exploration - Pictorial works. I. Title.

994.01

The State of Western Australia has made an investment
in this project through the Department for the Arts.

*No sea can hurt her ...*

Captain James Cook, 3 August 1771.

# ACKNOWLEDGEMENTS

Published in association with *Sunday Times* newspaper, Perth — Western Australia to coincide with the centenary celebrations, and with the assistance of H M Bark Endeavour Foundation.

Richard Polden would like to thank the following people: John Longley, Captain Chris Blake, Bill Repard, Lloyd Jones, Martin Saxon, Jeff and Judy Osborne, Gary and Sandra Merrin, Jeremy Toneman, Wally Strother, Colin Graham, and his family.

The publisher thanks Mike Lefroy, John Longley and Jenny Longley for their invaluable assistance with this project.

Extracts from Captain Cook's journals are taken from Volume I of *The Voyage of the Endeavour 1768-1771* edited by J C Beaglehole, published by Cambridge for the Hakluyt Society at the University Press, 1955.

Contemporary extracts are taken from the 'Captain's Reports' and 'Watch Reports' and are reproduced with permission of the H M Bark Endeavour Foundation.

# CONTENTS

Map                                          8

Foreword                                     9

The Voyage                                  10

Background                                 132

Specifications                             134

Crew List                                  135

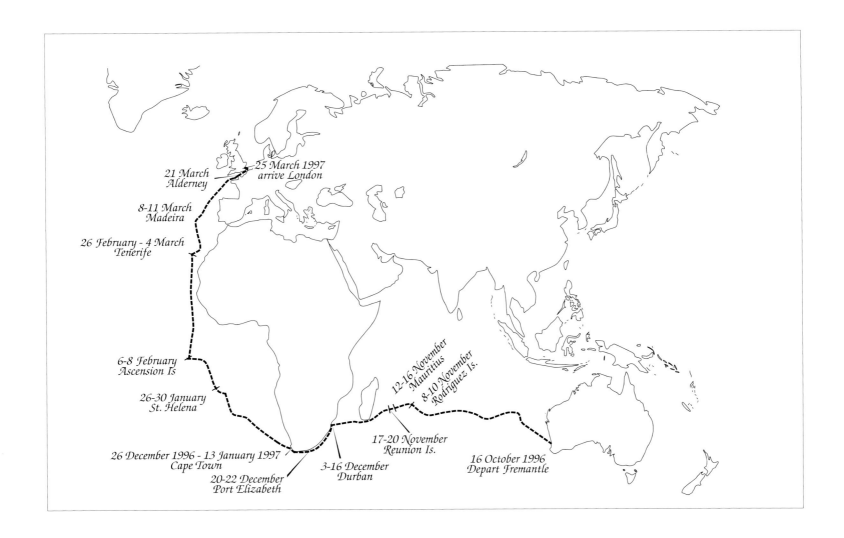

21 March
Alderney

25 March 1997
arrive London

8-11 March
Madeira

26 February - 4 March
Tenerife

6-8 February
Ascension Is

26-30 January
St. Helena

12-16 November
Mauritius

8-10 November
Rodriguez Is.

17-20 November
Reunion Is.

26 December 1996 - 13 January 1997
Cape Town

16 October 1996
Depart Fremantle

20-22 December
Port Elizabeth

3-16 December
Durban

Voyage of *Endeavour*
16 October 1996 – 25 March 1997
Fremantle to London.

# FOREWORD

The *Endeavour* story dates back to 1986, when the Trustees of the newly created Australian National Maritime Museum decided that a museum standard replica of Captain James Cook's famous ship should be built to interpret modern Australia's European roots.

It was an audacious plan and I am sure that not many of those who proposed it felt that the construction of such a ship would actually come to pass. But come to pass it did, and not as a watered down version of the original concept, but as something even greater.

The original idea was to build a ship on the shores of Sydney Harbour, that would be towed across to Darling Harbour to spend her life as a floating exhibit. The reality is a ship built capable of making unassisted, unlimited passages on the great ocean sailing routes of the world, while remaining faithful to the original concept of building a museum standard replica.

This book documents the first great voyage that *Endeavour* has undertaken — to sail to London from Fremantle, where she was built, via the Cape of Good Hope. A far cry from being towed across Sydney Harbour.

The story of how *Endeavour* was built and the work that has been done by her crew to develop the confidence of her Trustees to approve this great voyage, is a story that will be told elsewhere but in short is one of hundreds of men and women of all stations in life believing in the project and ultimately the ship.

It is the spirit of this great ship and her namesake HM Bark *Endeavour*, that has made this voyage possible. I think that when you look at Richard Polden's marvellous photographs, that spirit is clear for all to see.

John Longley, AM
Chief Executive Officer
HM Bark Endeavour Foundation Pty Ltd
Fremantle, January 1998

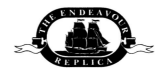

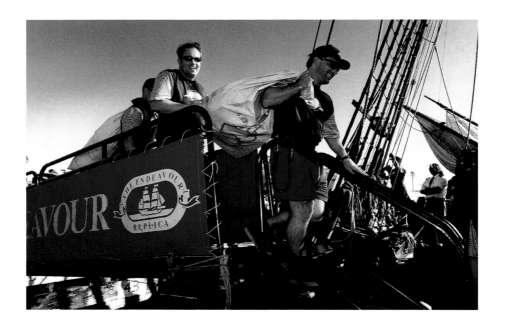

Much secrecy surrounds the preparation for departure from England of His Majesty's Bark, Endeavour. In view of extensive preparations being undertaken, your correspondent asks whether Scientific study is the only reason for the Voyage of the Endeavour. We have received Certain Information to the contrary.

London Gazette, 1768.

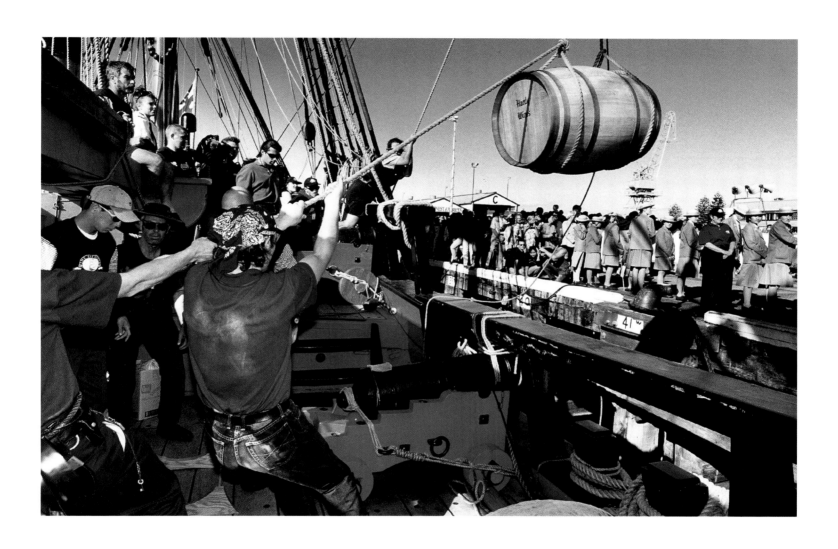

Hoisting a barrel of wine aboard.

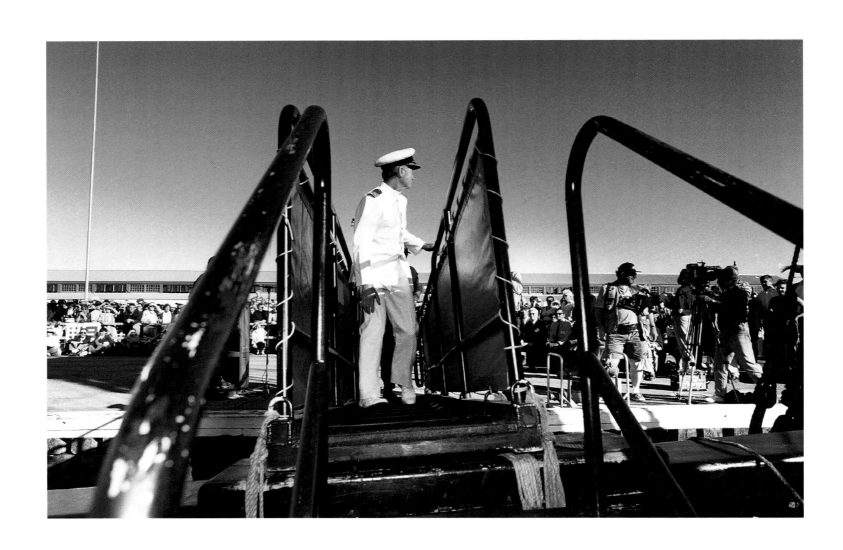

Captain Chris Blake boards *Endeavour*.

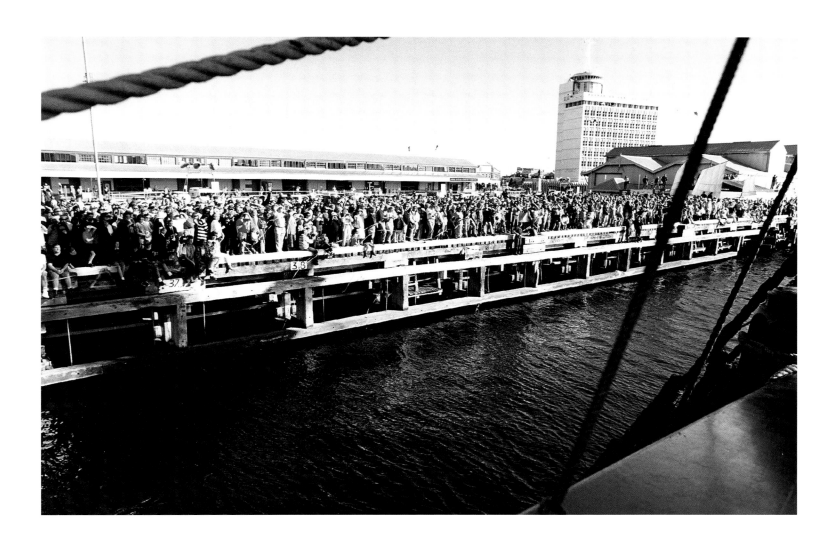

Farewelling *Endeavour*.

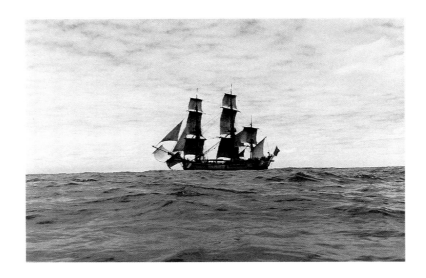

Wednesday had finally arrived. The tension was incredible. We were all called aboard and the gangway was removed. A gap of just a metre but it could have been miles.

We said goodbye to the Fremantle Hotel and waved farewell to the thousands of well wishers at Victoria Quay. The camera flashes and headlights of the cars flashing along the coastline provided us with an unforgettable memory of Perth and our last sight of land for a whole month.

At last we were on our own – a calmness and a sense of anticipation fell over us. We realised we were really underway. The following day we were on morning watch and had our first real experience of the ocean as the dawn broke and we were well out of sight of land. A view we will get well used to over the next month.

Crew member, 1996.

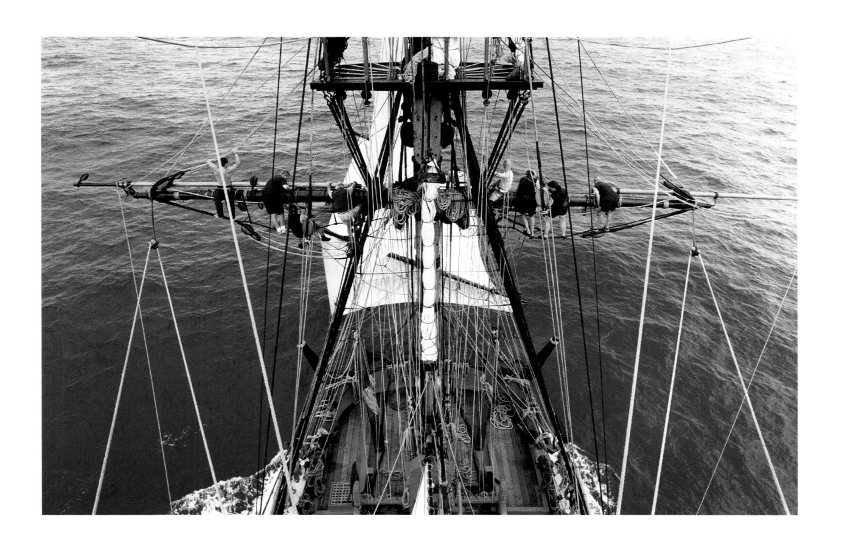

Crew members furling the course on the foremast.

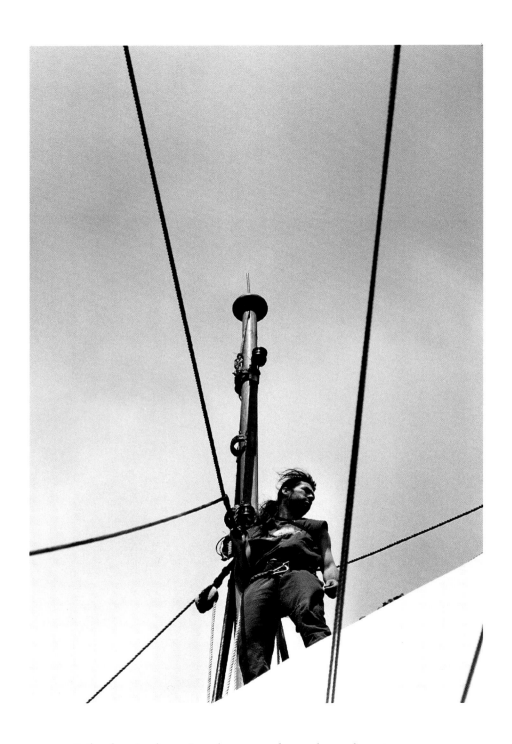

Sailmaker Anthony Longhurst stands watch on the mizzenmast.

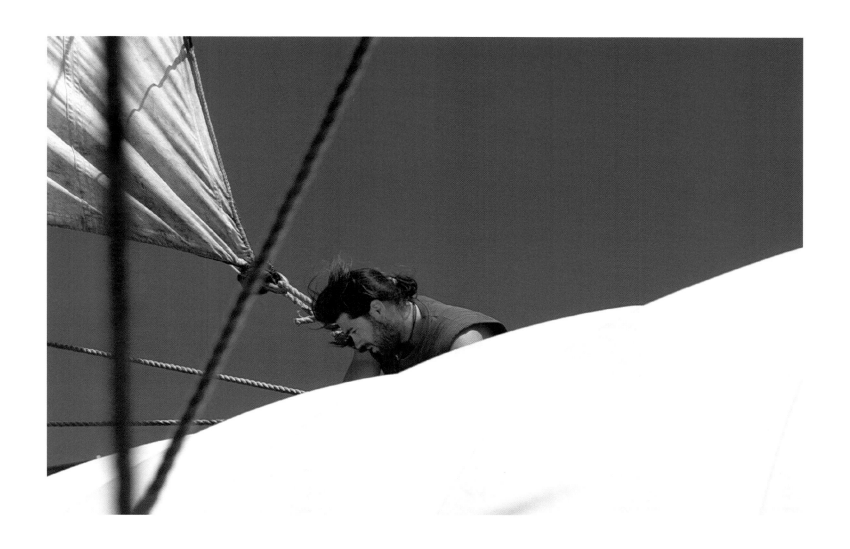

Anthony Longhurst under billowing canvas.

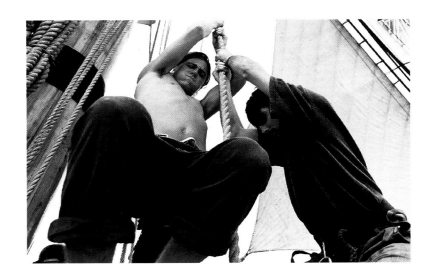

*We have now been at sea for twelve nights and are at an amusing stage where teasing, joking and mischievous pranks form a good part of our daily routine. However, it is not all sweetness and light. The ship's routine is demanding. We rouse, eat, clean, learn, eat once more, upkeep ship, eat again, keep watch and finally pipe down looking forward to exactly the same again for the next day, the day after that, and every other day except Sunday. Sunday on board is kept as a day of peace where there is a thoroughly relaxed atmosphere and comparatively little to do, except general watchkeeping.*

Calum Bennett, 1997.

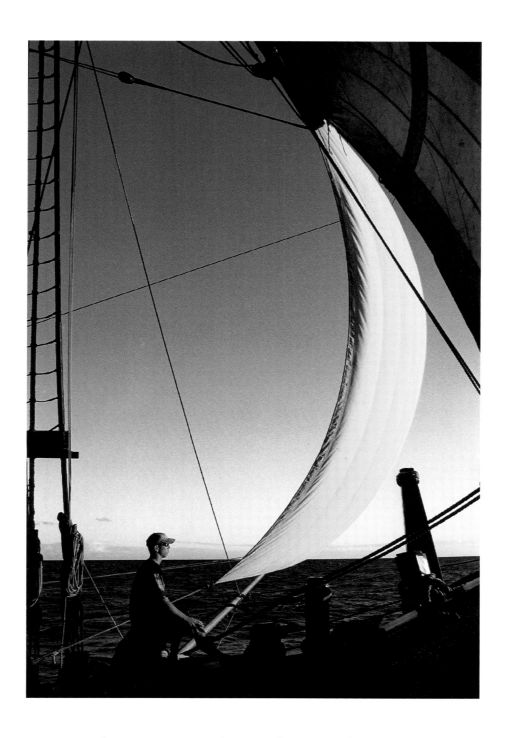

Jeremy Channon stares past the stunsail into an Indian Ocean sunset.

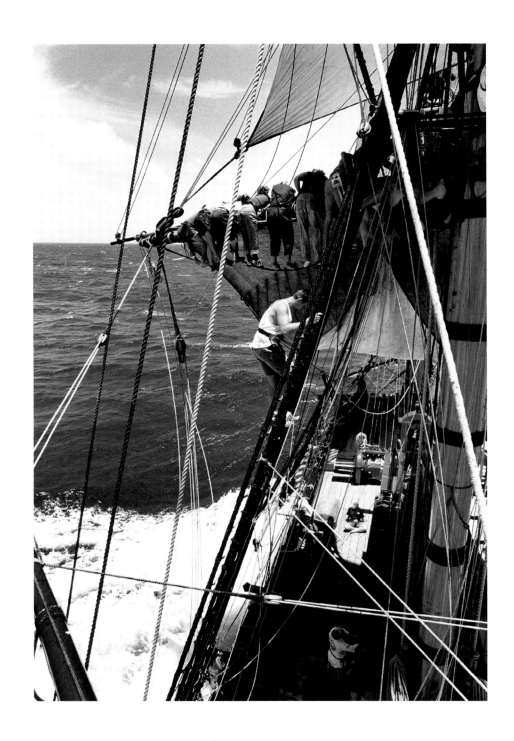

Reefing the main course.

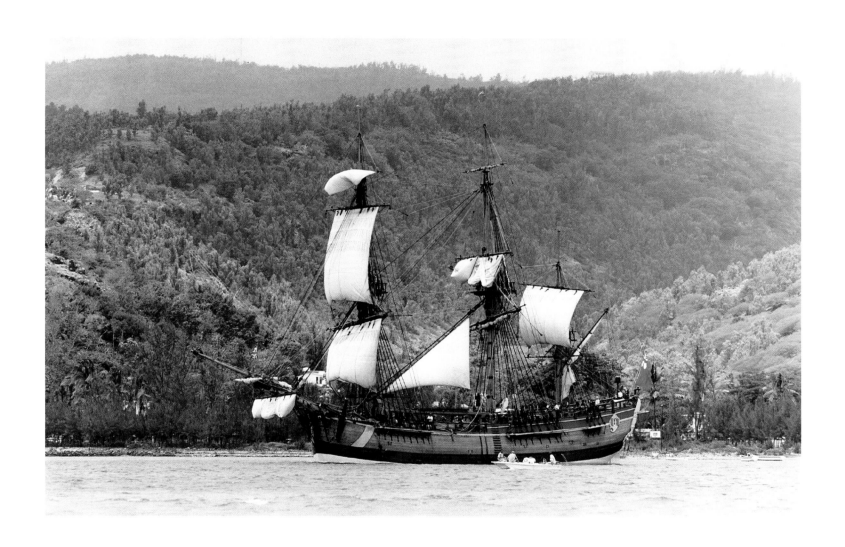

*Endeavour* leaves Rodrigues, a French protectorate in the Indian Ocean.

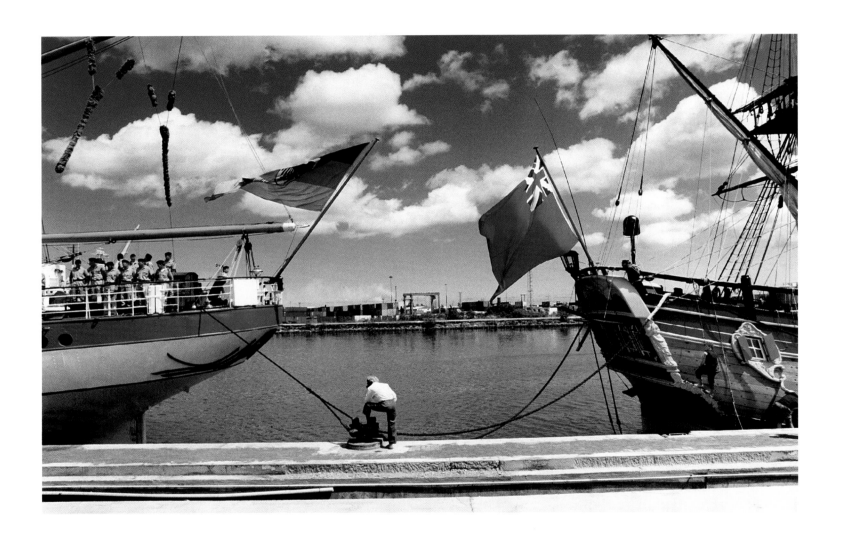

Sisters under sail: *Gorch Foch*, a German sail training vessel and *Endeavour* tie off to the same bollard at Port Louis, Mauritius.

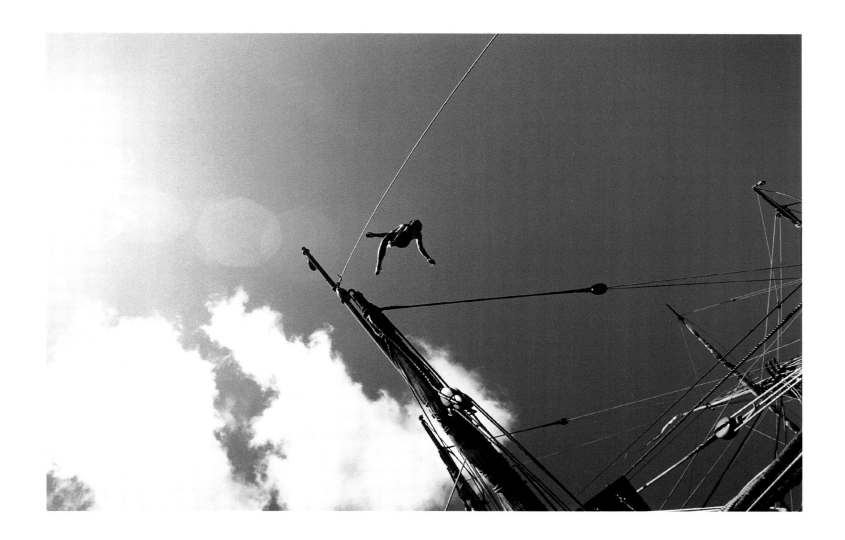

Diving from the yard.

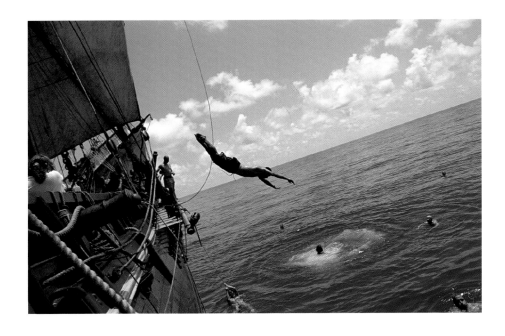

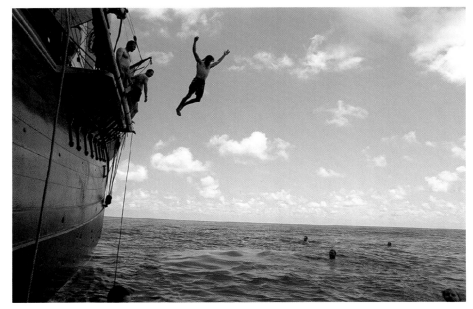

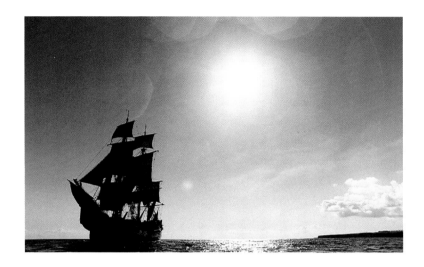

*With the heat of the sun, the temperature is stifling below deck. There have been a couple of opportunities to cool off in the afternoon when we were able to dive over the side for a swim. It was sheer bliss, but never quite long enough!*

Helen Charlesworth, 1997.

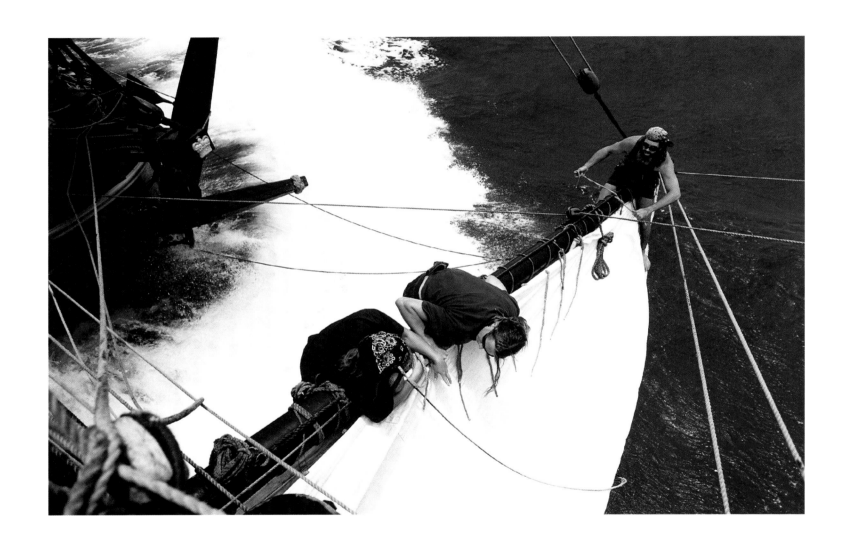

Reefing the spritsail.

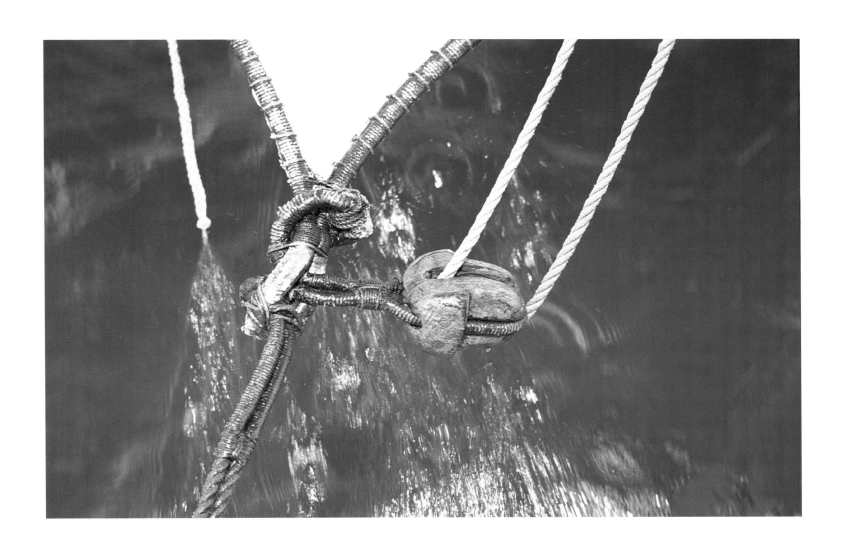

The spritsail clew breaks the blue ocean.

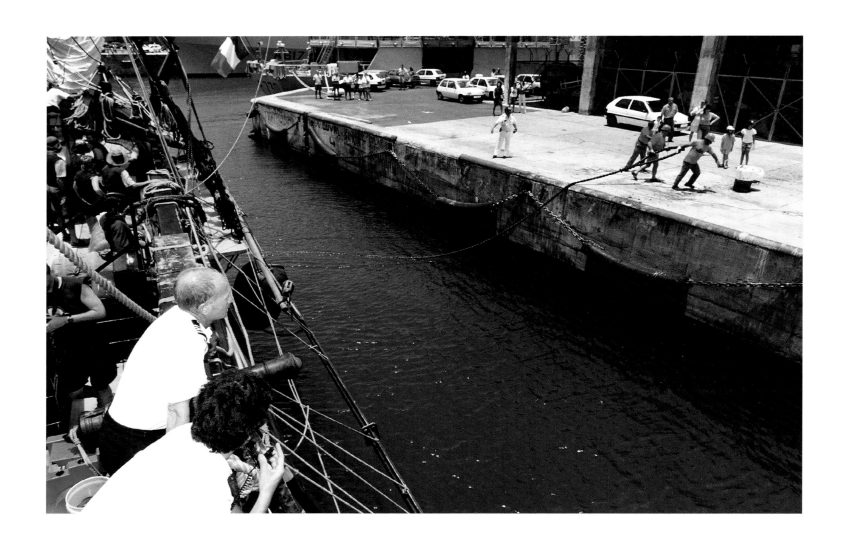

Berthing operations at Port St Denis, Reunion Island.

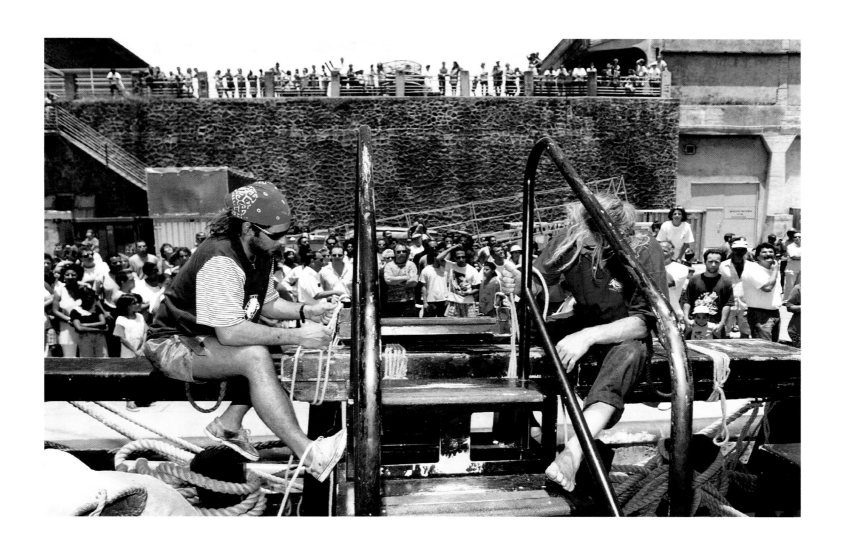

Rigging the gangway, Reunion Island.

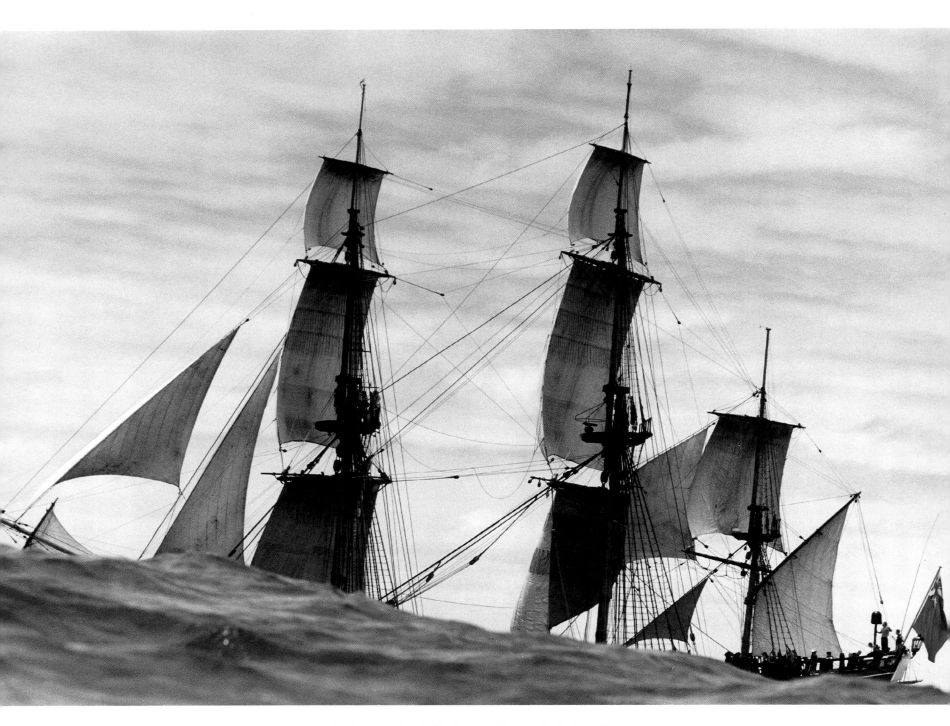

*Endeavour*, her hull obscured by swell, Indian Ocean.

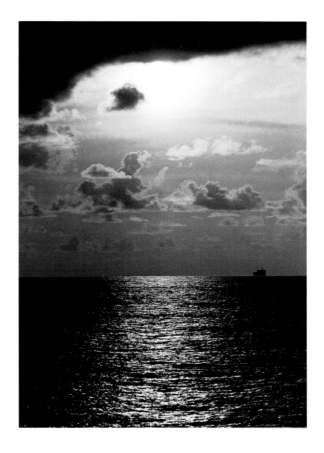

The moon rose from the east, full in all its glory, beaming its rays of enchantment over the ocean as it ascended through the clouds. As the clouds cleared, this magnificent ship was belted by moon glow, shimmering like the thousands of flash bulbs emanating from City Beach all those days ago.

The scene was one of pristine serenity for those who experienced it. I think we could sail 1500 miles to see it again.

Anna Rothwell, 1996.

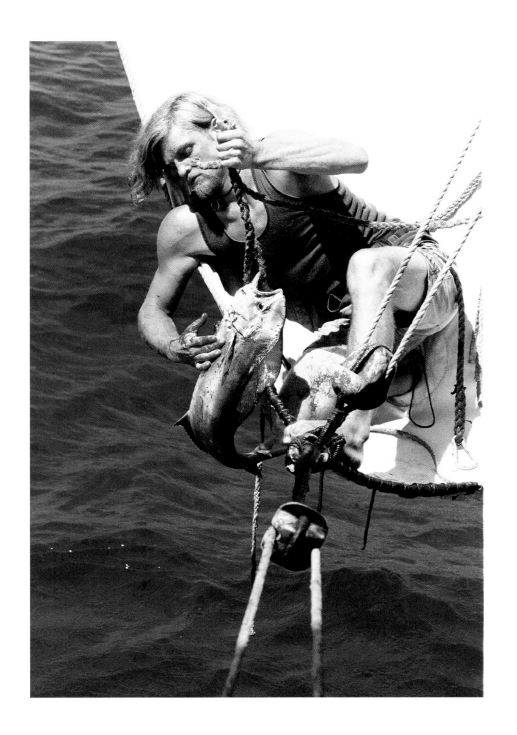

Perched on the spritsail clew, Gavin Reid hauls in a dorado.

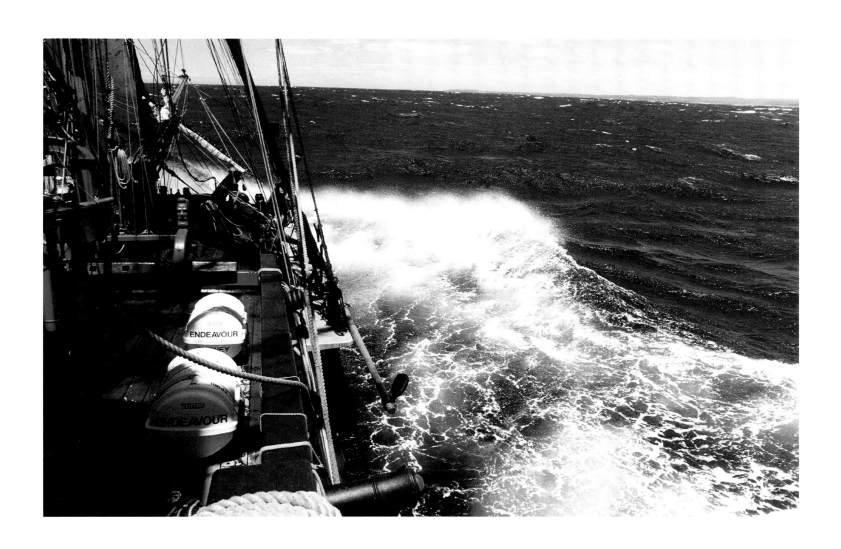

*Endeavour* ploughs through the deep off Durban.

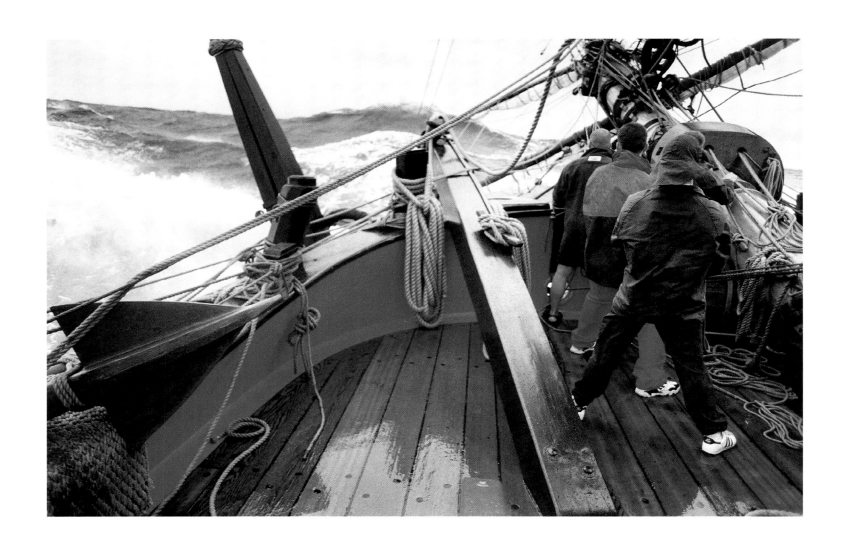

Rounding the Cape of Good Hope.

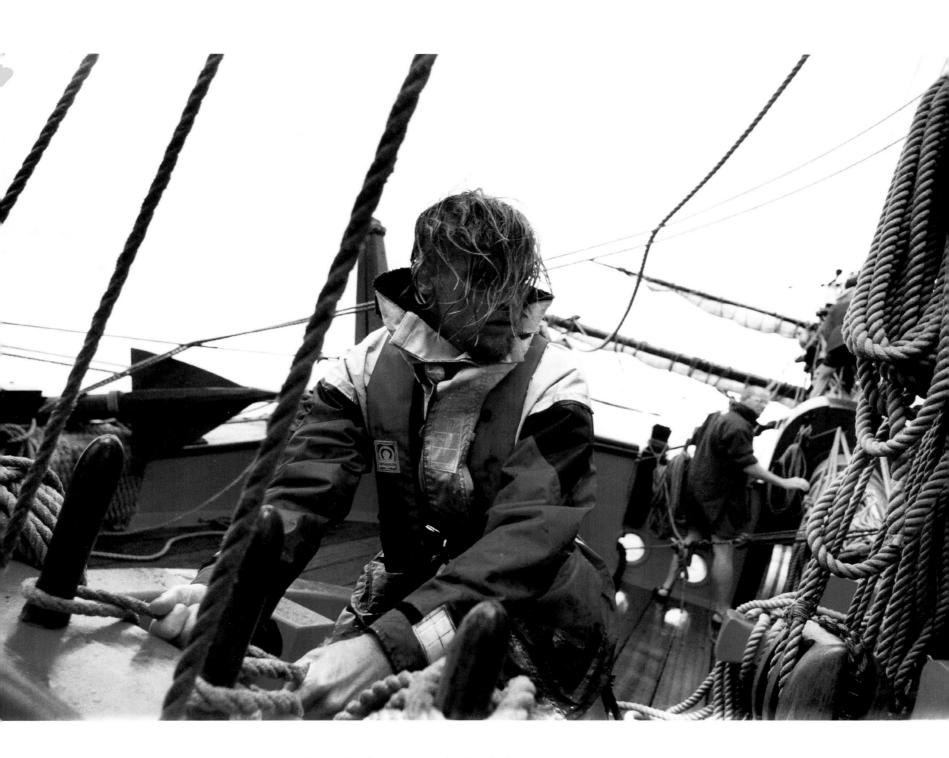

Gavin Reid at work on the foredeck in heavy weather.

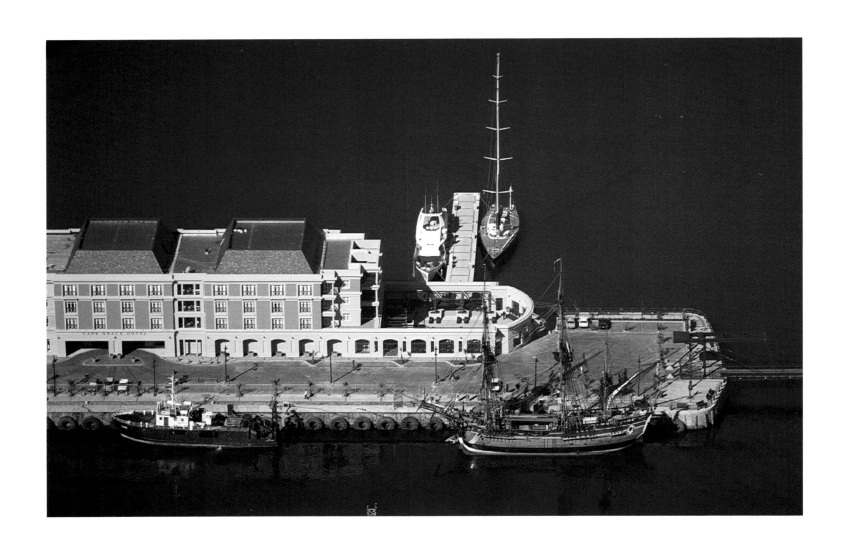

Snug alongside the waterfront in Cape Town.

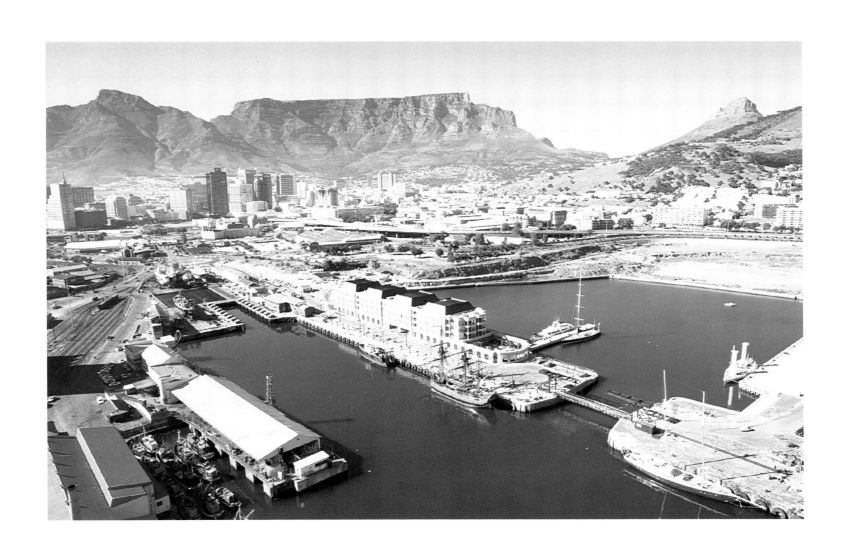

Table Mountain, Cape Town.

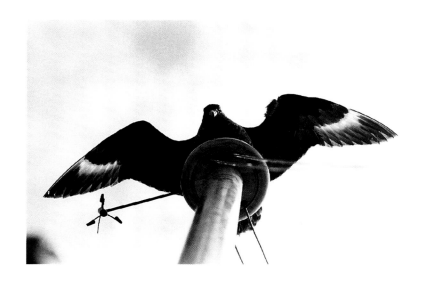

*Light gentle breezes and clear settled weather. PM saw on of the same sort of Birds as we saw last Saturday, these Birds are of a dark brown or Chocolate colour with some white feathers under their wings and are as big as ravens. Mr Gore says they are in great plenty at Port Egmont in Faulkland Islds, and for that reason calls them Port Egmont Hens. Saw a great many Porposes large and small the small ones had White bellies and noses. AM saw 2 Port Egmont Hens a seal, some Sea weed and a piece of wood, with Barnacles upon it*

Captain James Cook, 1769.

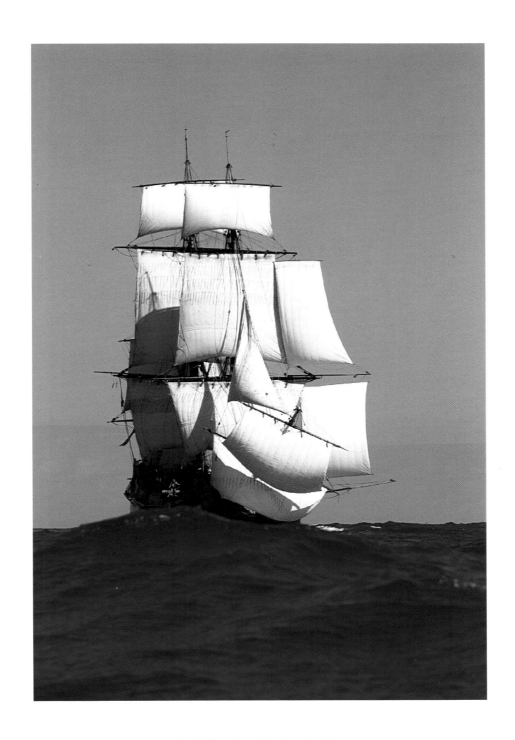

Under full sail in the South Atlantic.

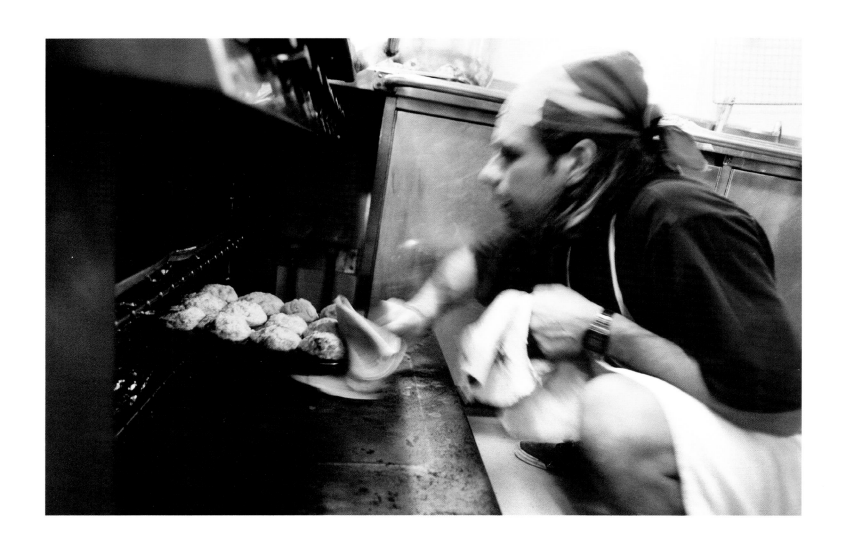

Richard Warnett, Cook's Mate, at speed in the galley.

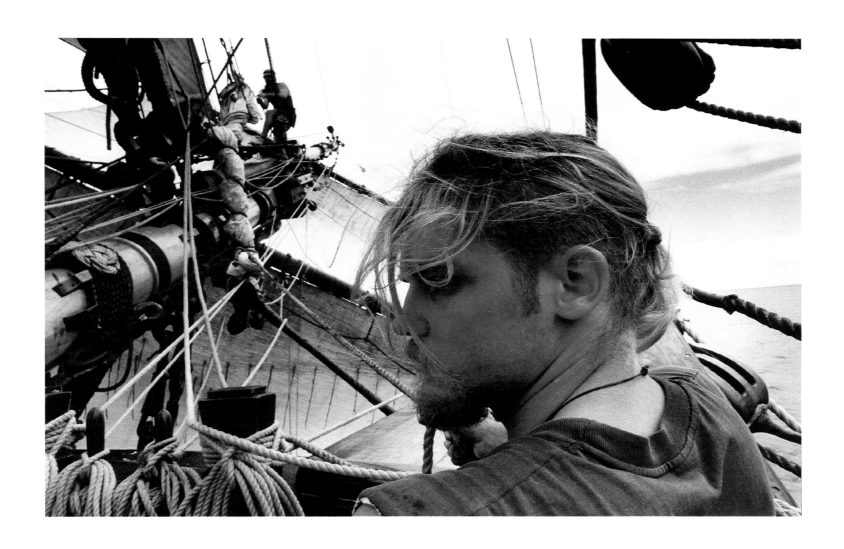

Gavin Reid, Bosun's Mate.

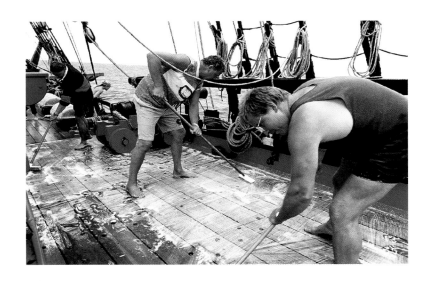

We are all finding that there is very little time in the day for recreation, due to the ongoing watch duties, cleaning and galley duties. What time there is left is spent writing letters, journals, washing and, most important of all, sleeping. Apart from cleaning out the toilets (or heads as they are referred to on a ship) and showers, cleaning thick, black tar from the ship's deadeyes before they can be painted, and spreading a thick grease known as tallow by hand on various parts of the rigging where chaffing occurs, have rated as the messiest jobs to date.

Andy Webb, 1997.

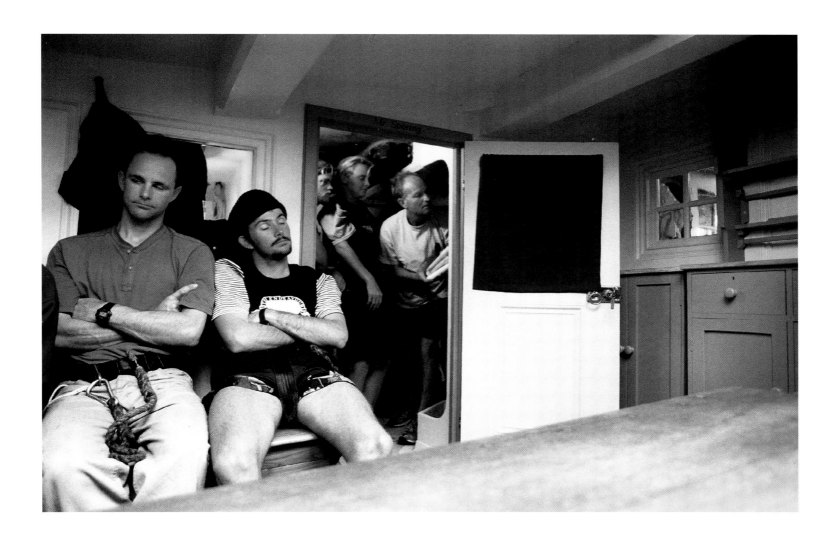

Two exhausted crewmen snatch a nap as the Captain carries out his weekly inspection.

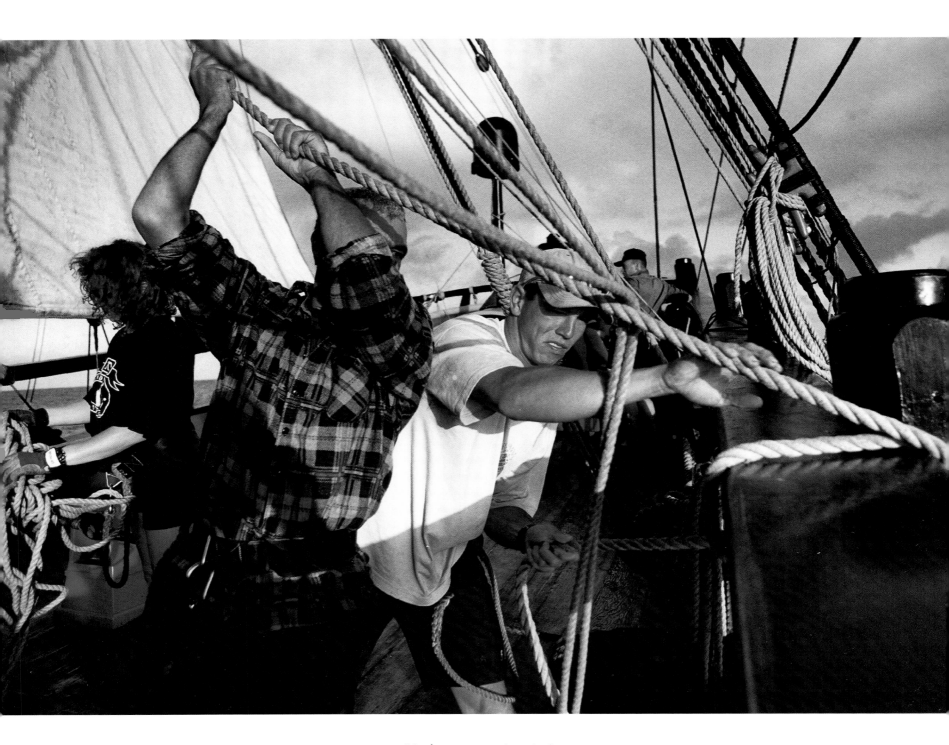

Hauling on running rigging.

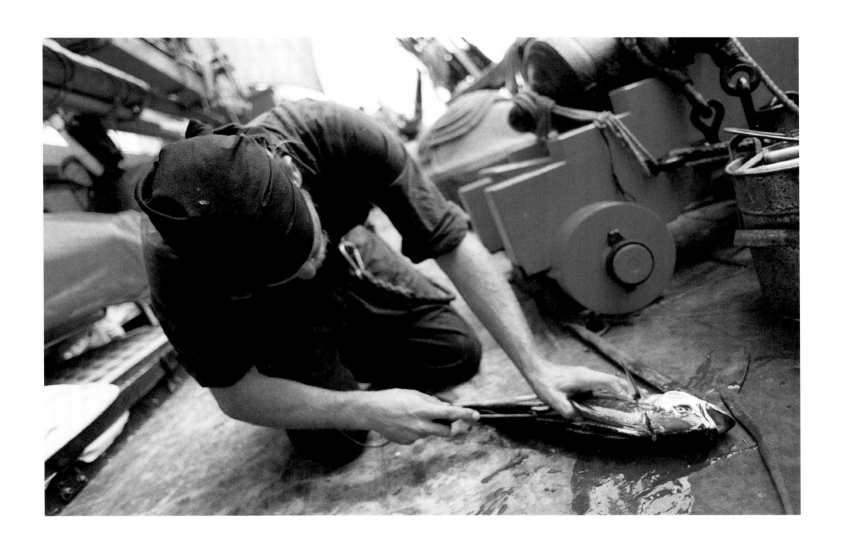

Catch of the day.

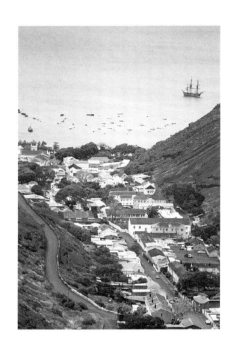

*Napoleon could not have wished for a finer place to have been banished. Jacob's Ladder led up the hill where the first of the infamous cricket matches were played. The school kids of St Helena may never forget the 'stacks on' as the 'hill' expressed their support for each and every player, and the chant of Ooh Aah An-Ton-ee still rang in the air as we prepared for a dance. The Saints shall be hard to forget.*

Calum Bennett, 1996.

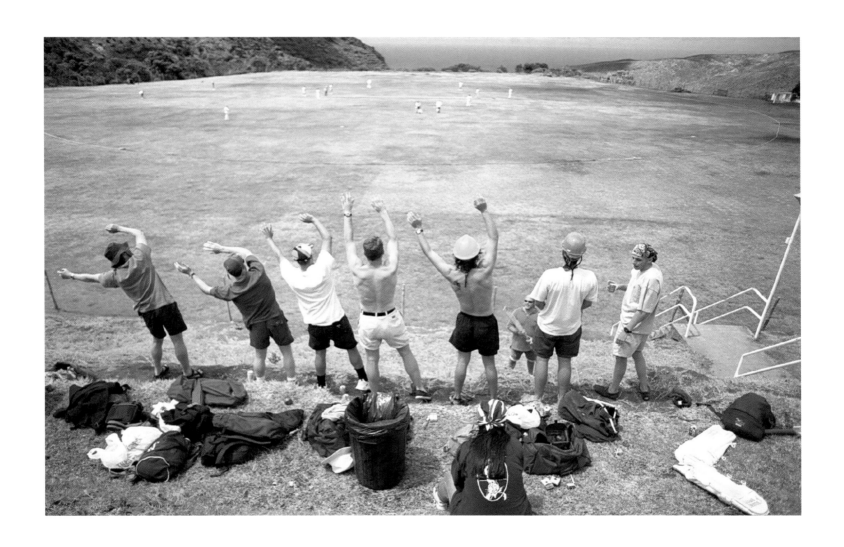

The *Endeavour* versus the Saints, St Helena cricket match.

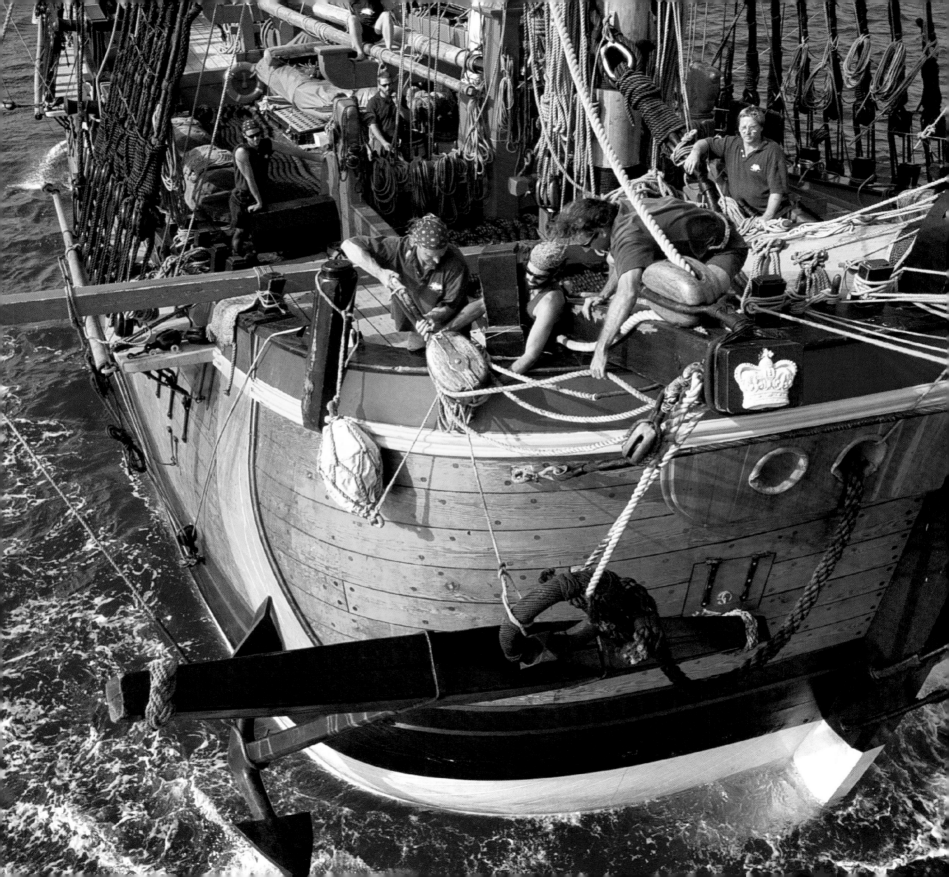

Opposite page: Slade Morgan, Anthony Longhurst and Scott Fell-Smith prepare to lower the best bower off Ascension Island while Danny McDermott stands by to assist.

*Endeavour* anchored off Ascension Island.

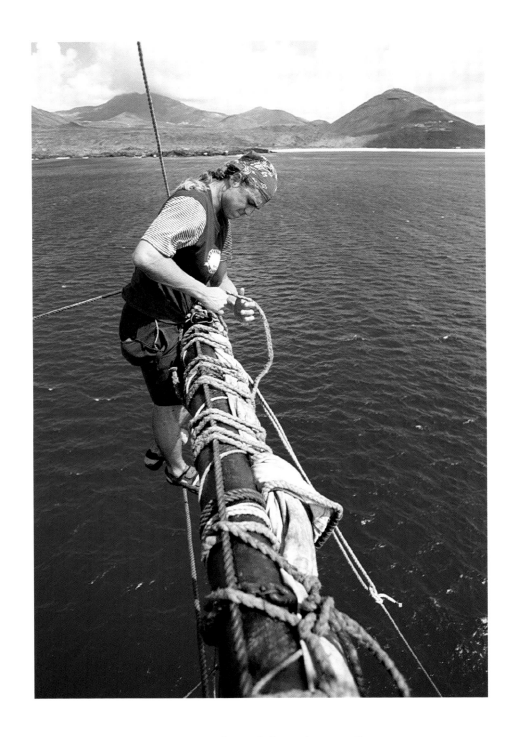

Ben Totty working aloft on the topgallant.

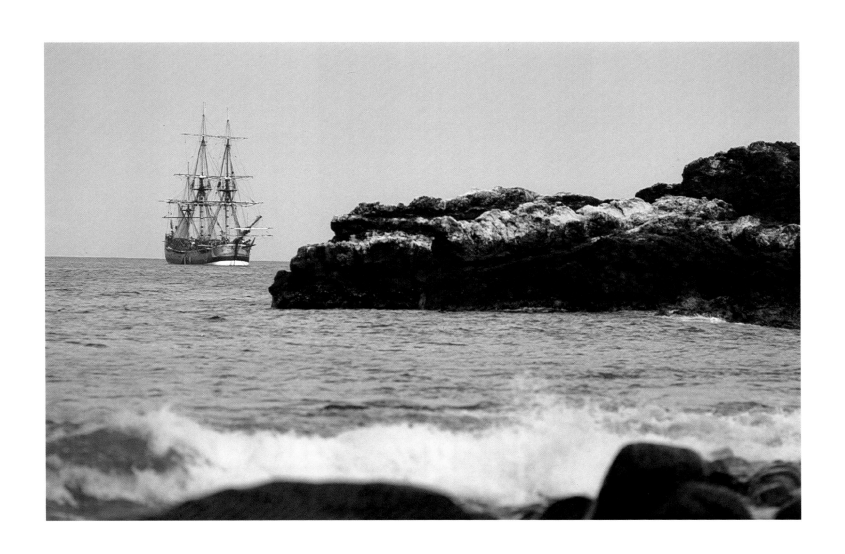

*Endeavour* anchored off Ascension Island.

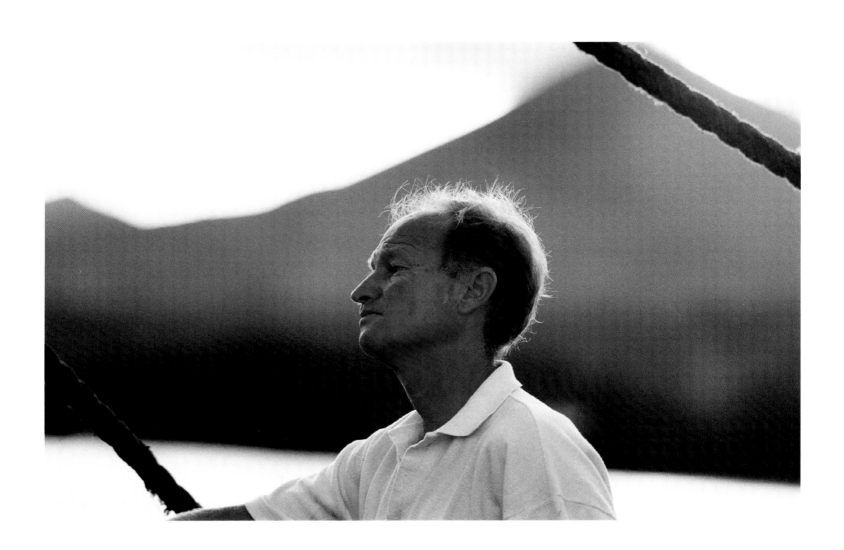

Captain Chris Blake, Ascension Island.

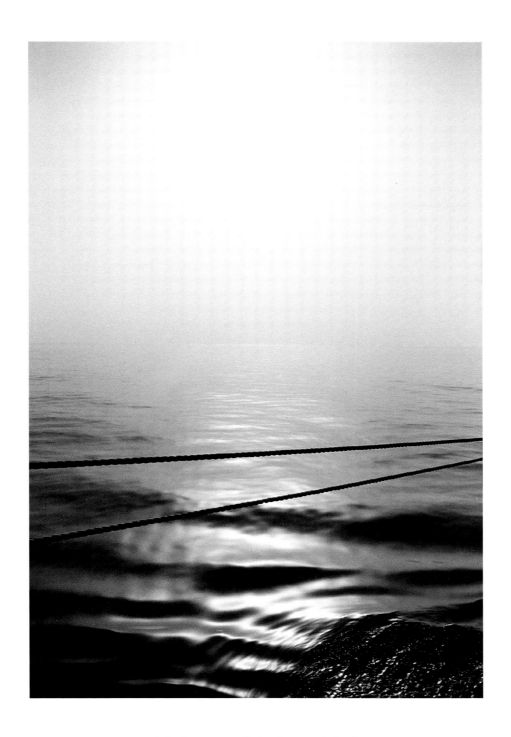

Mid-afternoon off the Canary Islands.

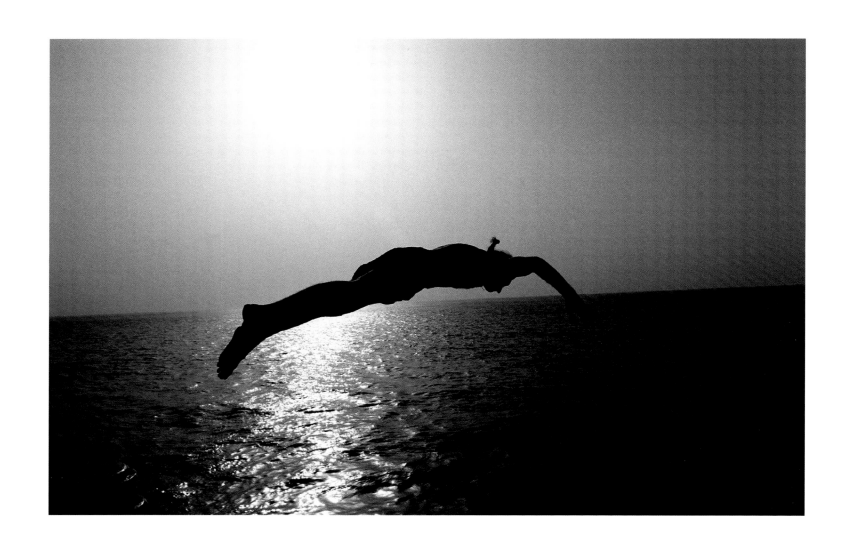

Scott Fell-Smith, deep sea diver.

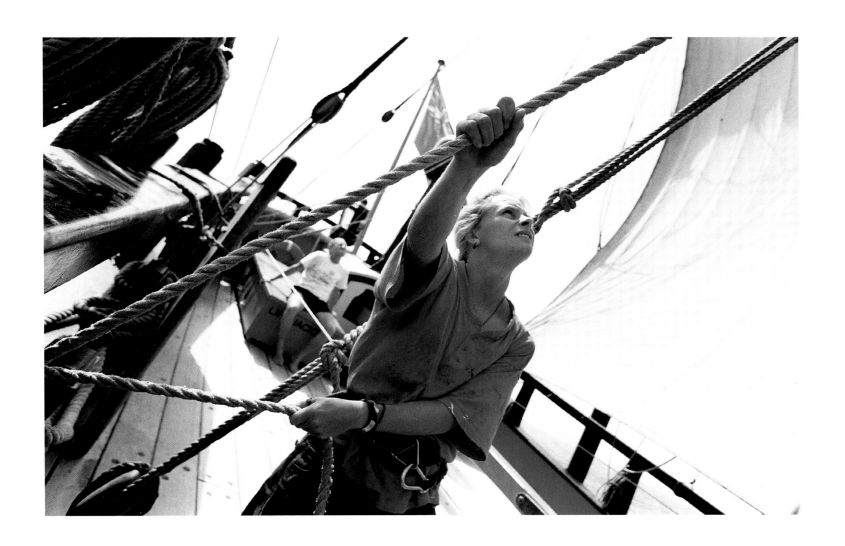

Christina Jackson trims the sails.

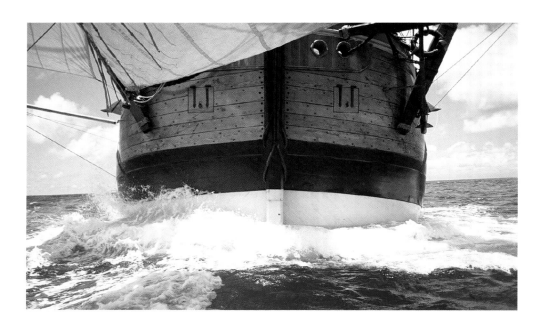

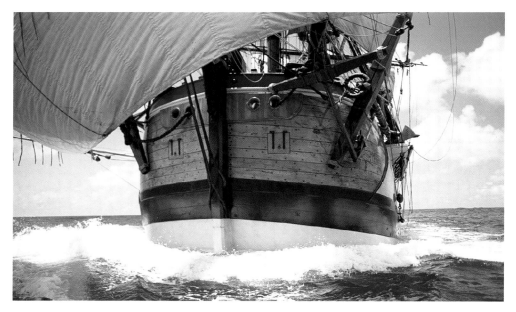

Heading for Tenerife.

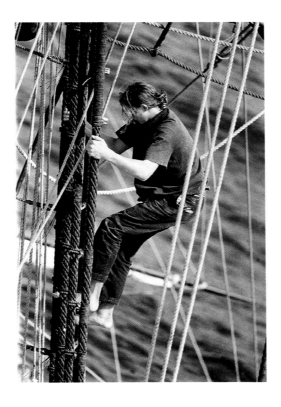

For me, the most important goal to get out of the way was the long climb to the top of the Mainmast, which is 39.27m from the main deck. I chose not to look down during the climb and when I reached the point where the yard meets the mast, I clipped on my safety line and edged out to the end of the yard. When all four crew were in position, we lunged at the sail together, with our arms stretched out, and grabbed as much canvas as possible and hauled it to the yard, then again and again until it was between our stomachs and the yard. We then hauled up the sail more neatly and secured it to the yard using the gasket lines. Finally came the long climb down, after a quick look around. Despite being a long way up, it wasn't really that bad!

Andy Webb, 1997.

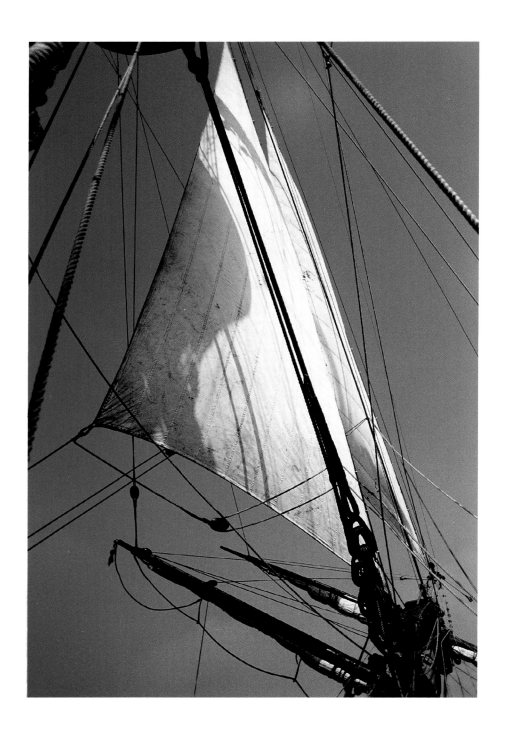

Light and shadows play on the head sails.

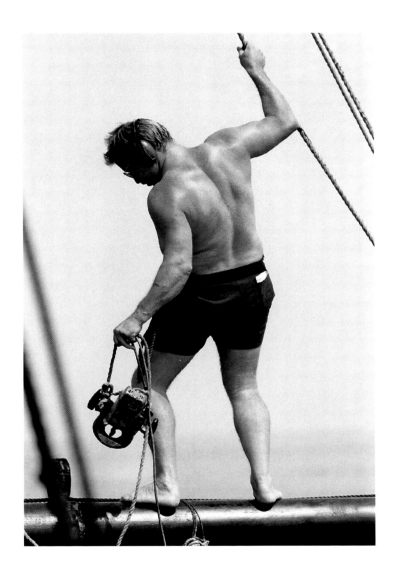
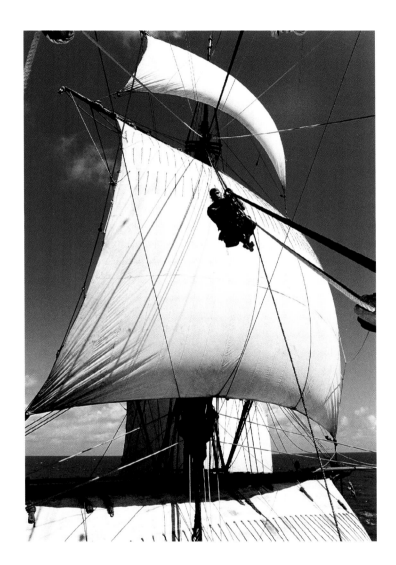

Left: Shipwright Danny McDermott walks to work along the main course yard. Right: Tarring the rigging.

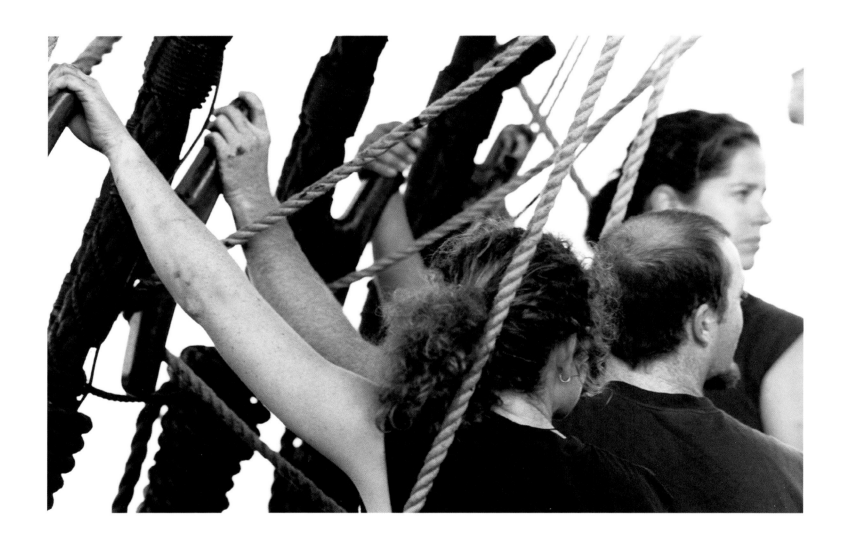

Crew await further orders during a sail handling maneuver.

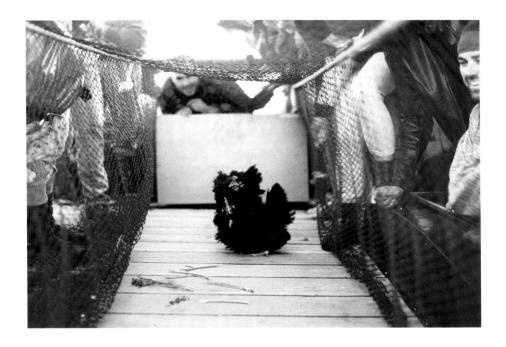

*Saturday was a big day on board with the Kentucky Chicken Derby being run. On deck we constructed our track and the chickens started off in the box and came out to the cheer of the crowd. Unfortunately they weren't attuned to this racing scene and grouped together, shuffling backwards and forwards at a painfully slow pace. 'Attila the Hen', 'Maggie Hatcher' 'The Bastard' and 'Tandoori Queen' were the contestants, with 'The Bastard' victorious.*

Crew member, 1996.

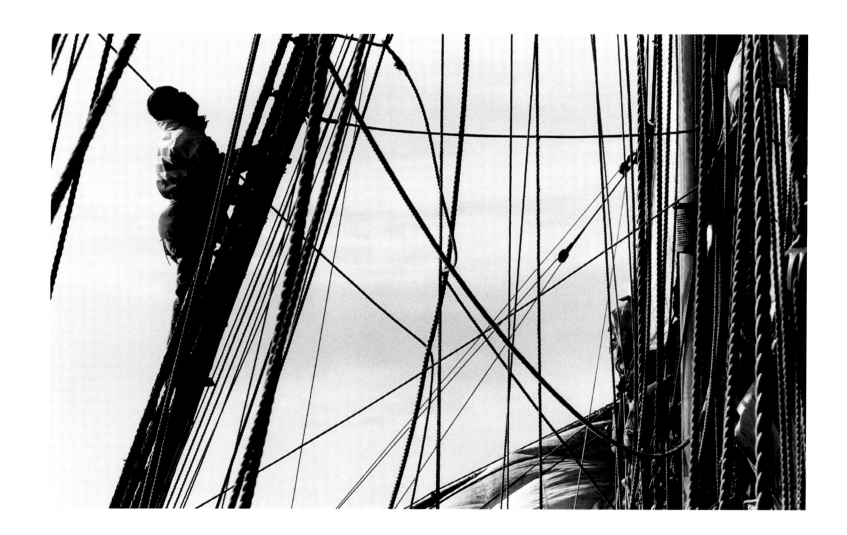

Aloft.

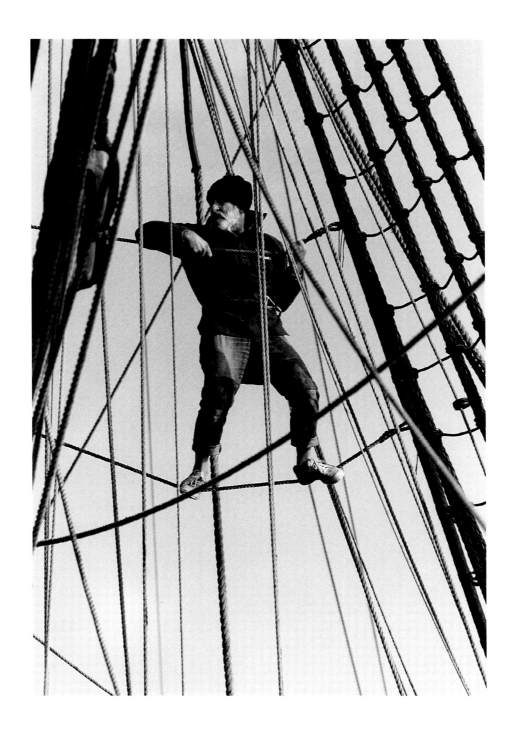

Tony Fowler in the rigging.

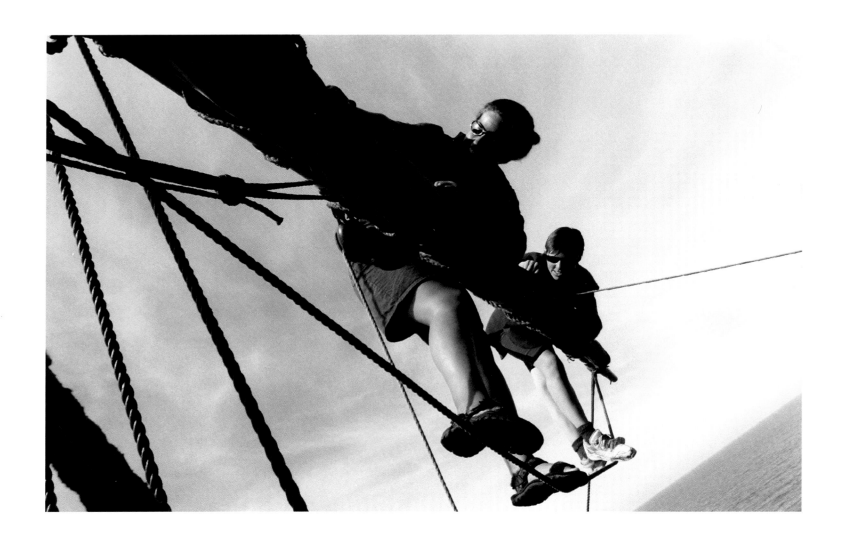

Debbie Wilson and Anna Brownlie furl the topgallant far above the deck.

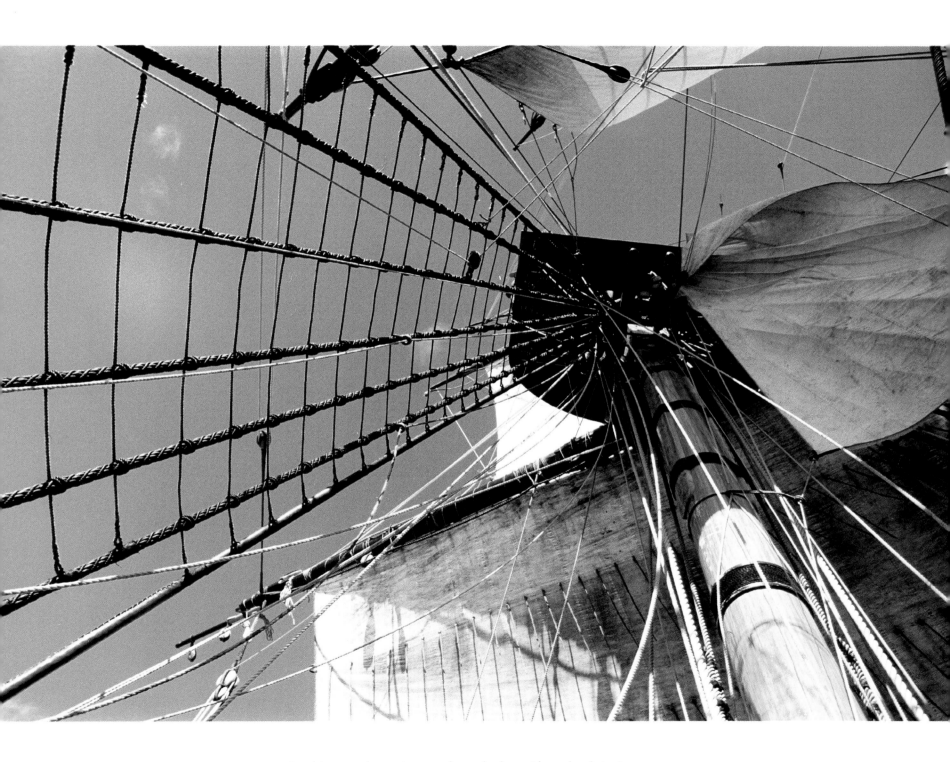

Looking up the mainmast through the spiderweb of rigging.

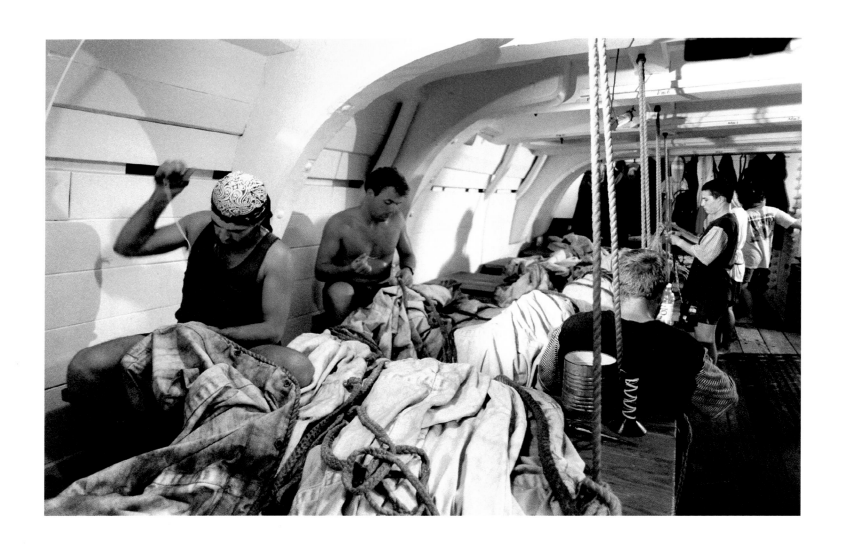

Repairing the mainsail below decks.

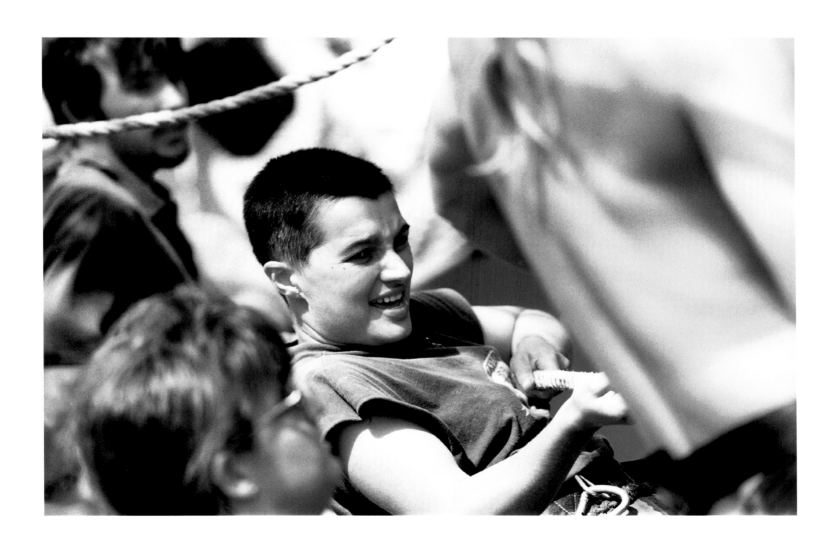

Zoe Egan lends a hand.

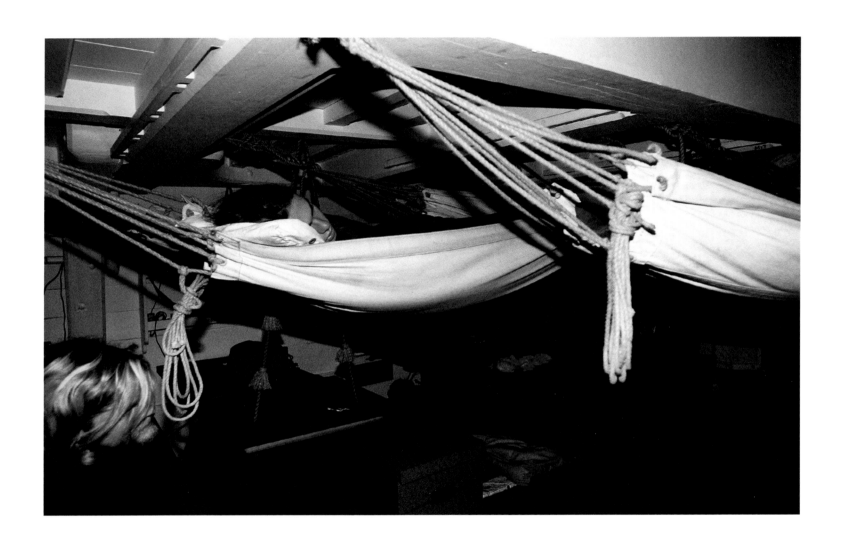

Lights out below decks.

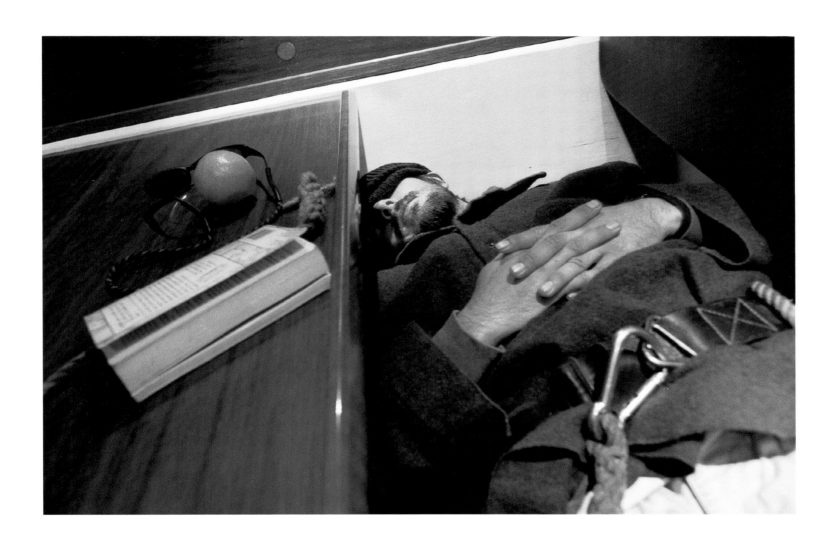

Exhausted.

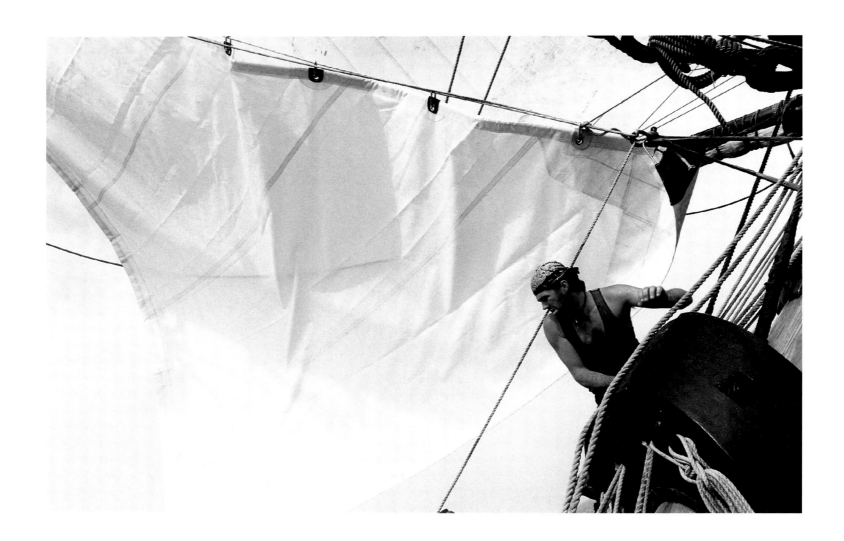

Anthony Longhurst tests a modern storm sail on the bowsprit.

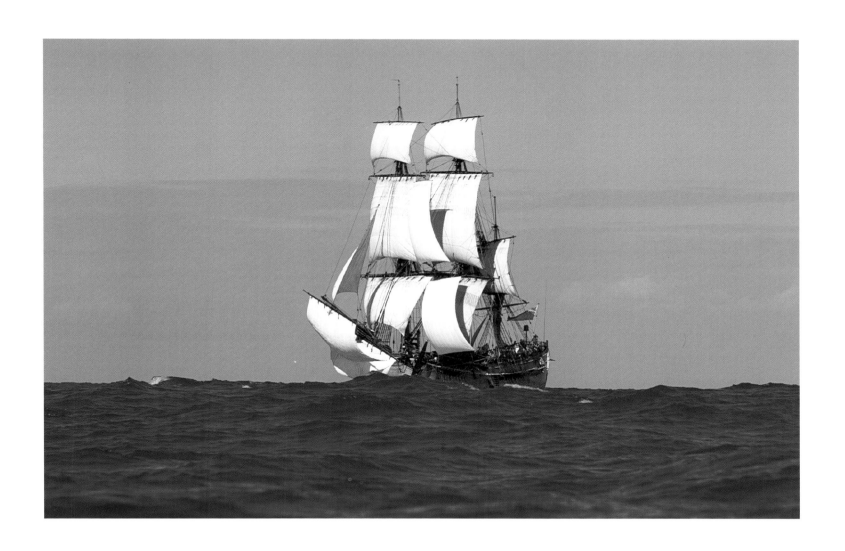

*Endeavour* under full sail.

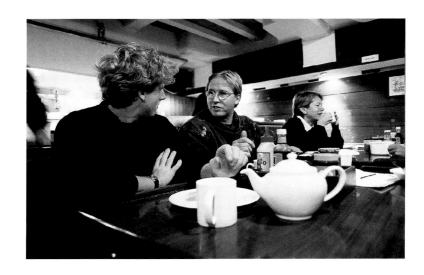

*We took Obarea's dog and had him immidiatly dress'd by some of the Natives in the following manner. They first made a hole in the ground in which they made a fire and heated some Stones, while this was doing the Dog was Strangle'd and the hair got off by laying him frequently upon the fire, his entrails were taken out and the whole washed clean, and as soon as the stones and hole was sufficiently heated, the fire was put out, and part of the Stones were left in the bottom of the hole, upon these Stones were laid Green leaves and upon them the Dog together with the entrails. These were likewise cover'd with leaves over them hot stones, and then the hole was close cover'd with mould: after he had laid there for about 4 hours, the Dog taken out whole and well done, and it was the opinion of every one who taisted of it that they Never eat sweeter meat, we therefore resolved for the future not to despise Dogs flesh.*

Captain James Cook, 1769.

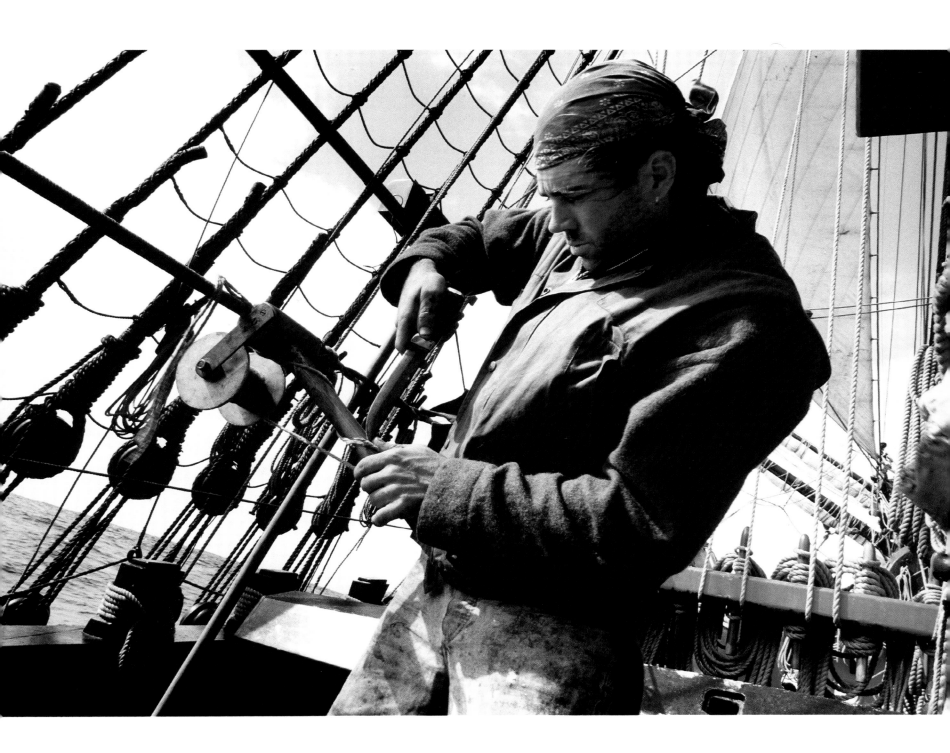
Anthony Longhurst serves a rope to prevent chaffing.

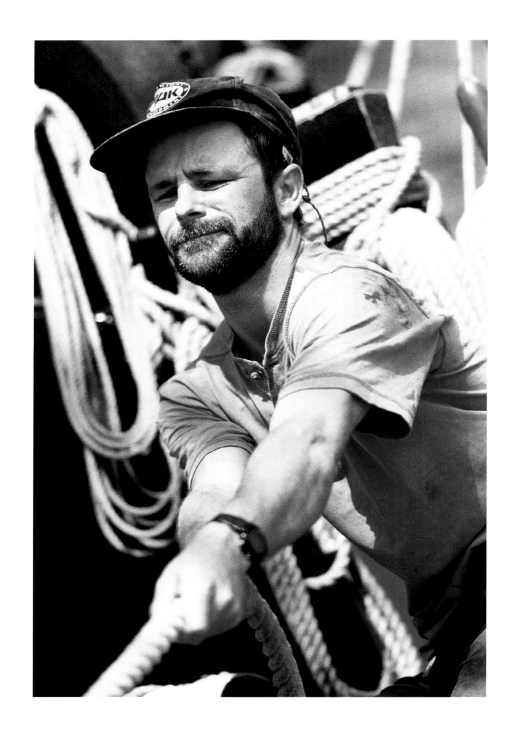

Crewman Andy 'Spider' Webb hauls home a sheet.

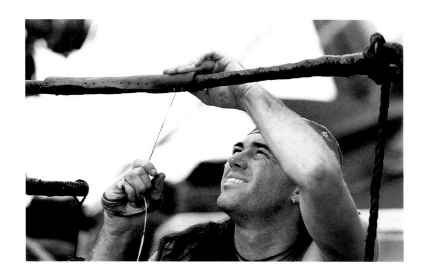

*Despite all the work each day, it's tremendously enjoyable. I am no literary expert, but I would be amazed if there were words which could describe the continual work accurately, and, at the same time, portray the extent of completely and utterly unexplainable enjoyment. Perhaps that's just sailing.*

Calum Bennett, 1997.

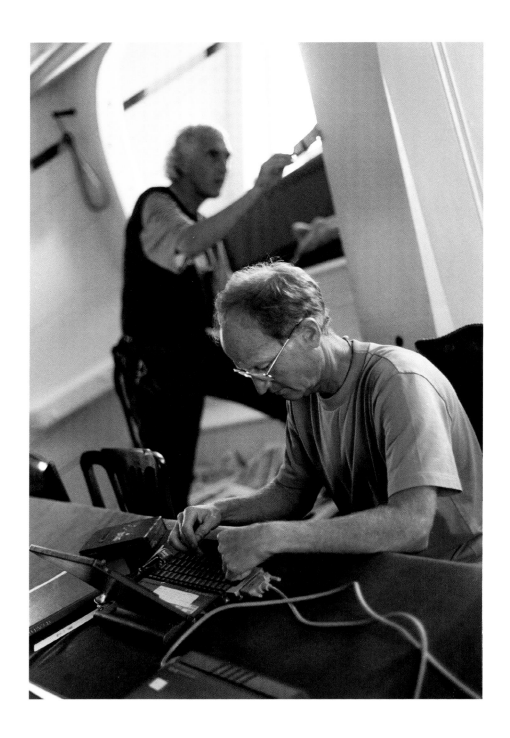

The Captain communicating with the 20th century in the Great Cabin.

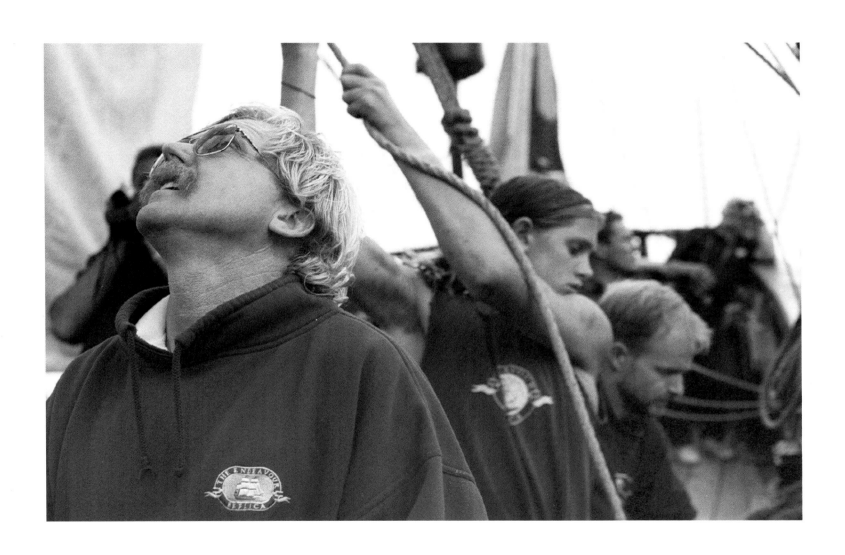

First Mate Geoff Kerr (foreground) supervises crew working the sails.

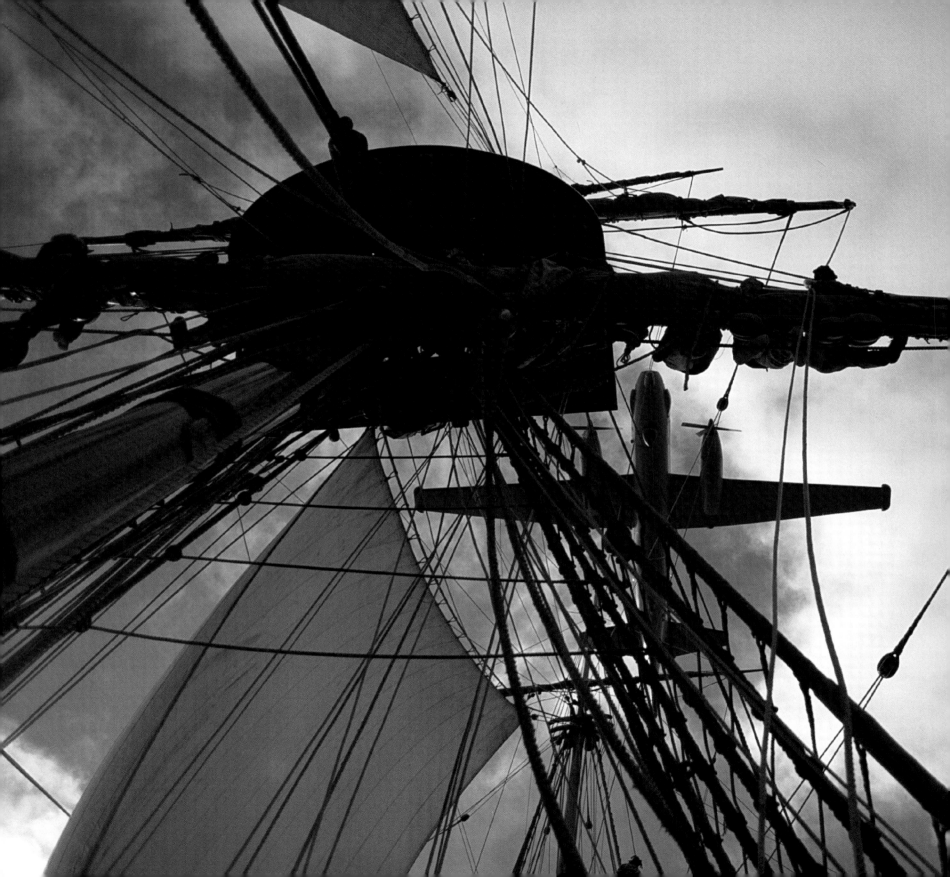

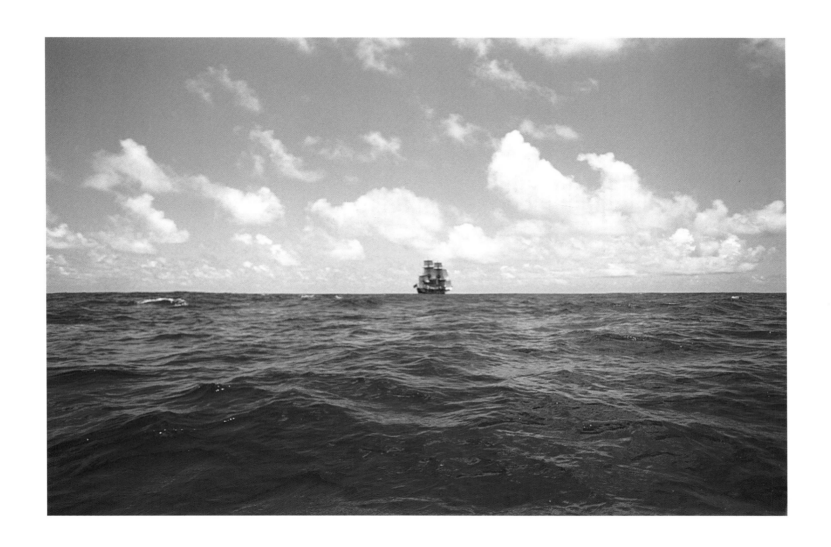

Opposite page: A long-range marine surveillance aircraft flies over *Endeavour*.

Mid ocean

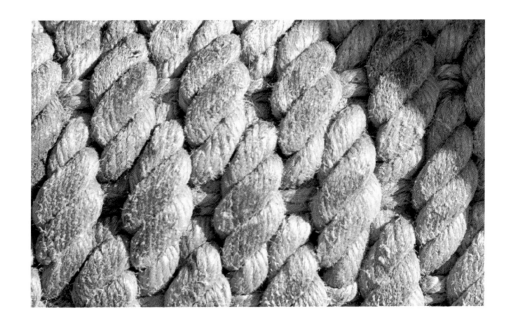

*The crew have continually been on the look out for chafe and wear of the gear (standing and running rigging) and 'chafing pads' have been placed on the most sensitive areas. Both the fore and main topsail jeer lines have been wormed and served.*

Captain Chris Blake, 1996.

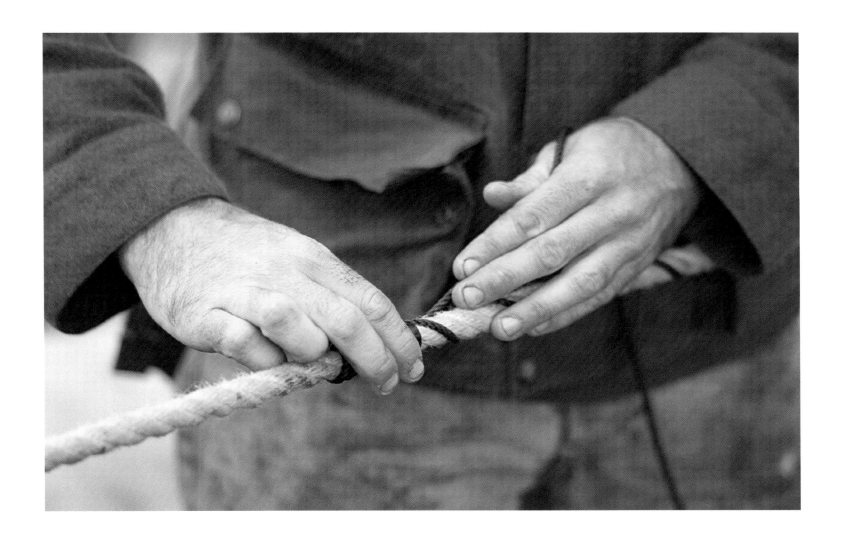

Worming the rope — the first step in the process of protecting rope from the elements.

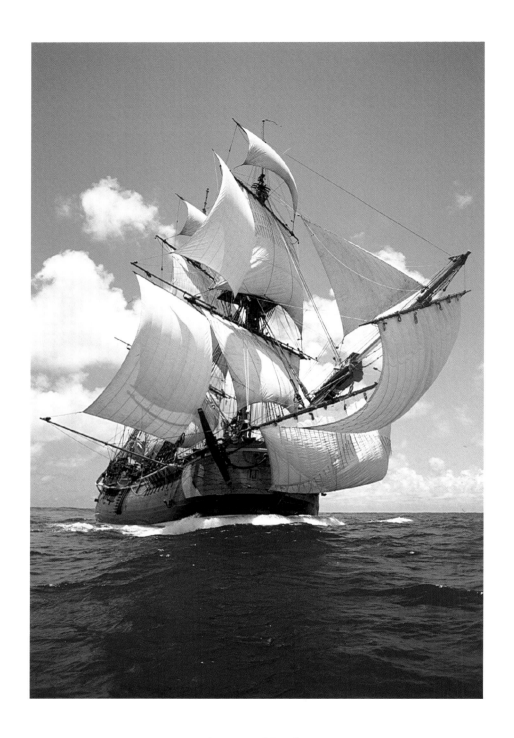

Making good headway.

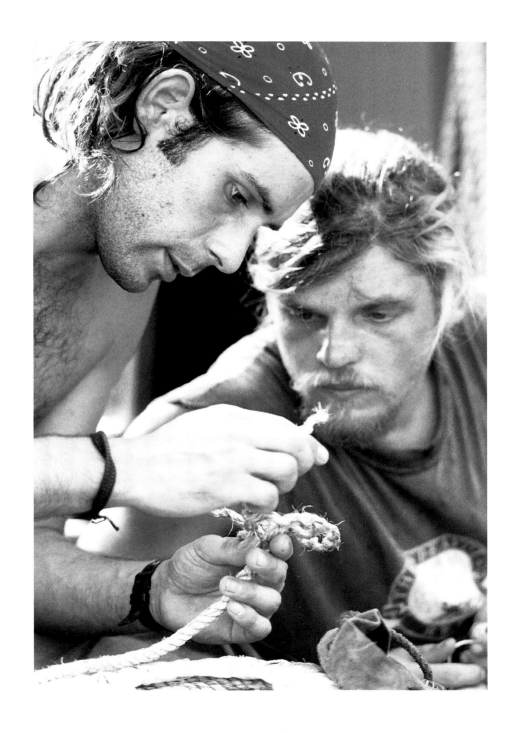

Richard Warnett and Gavin Reid.

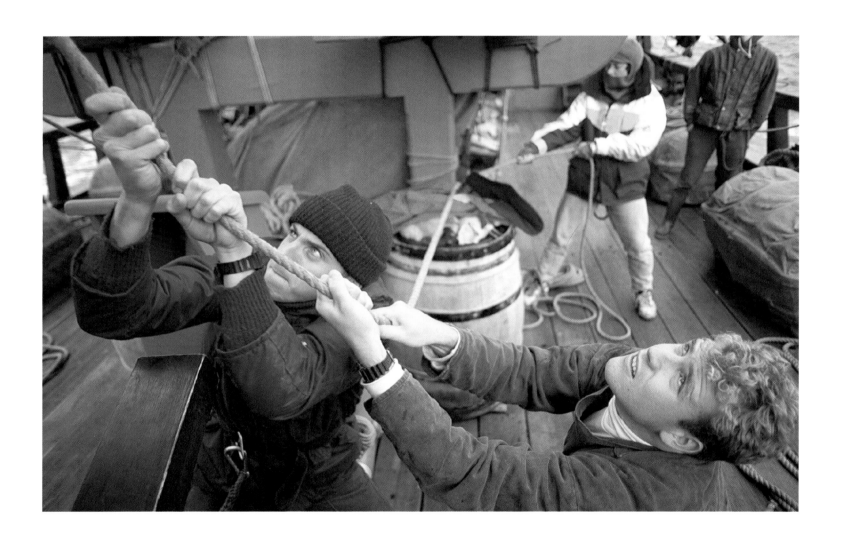

All eyes aloft as crew alter sails in rough weather.

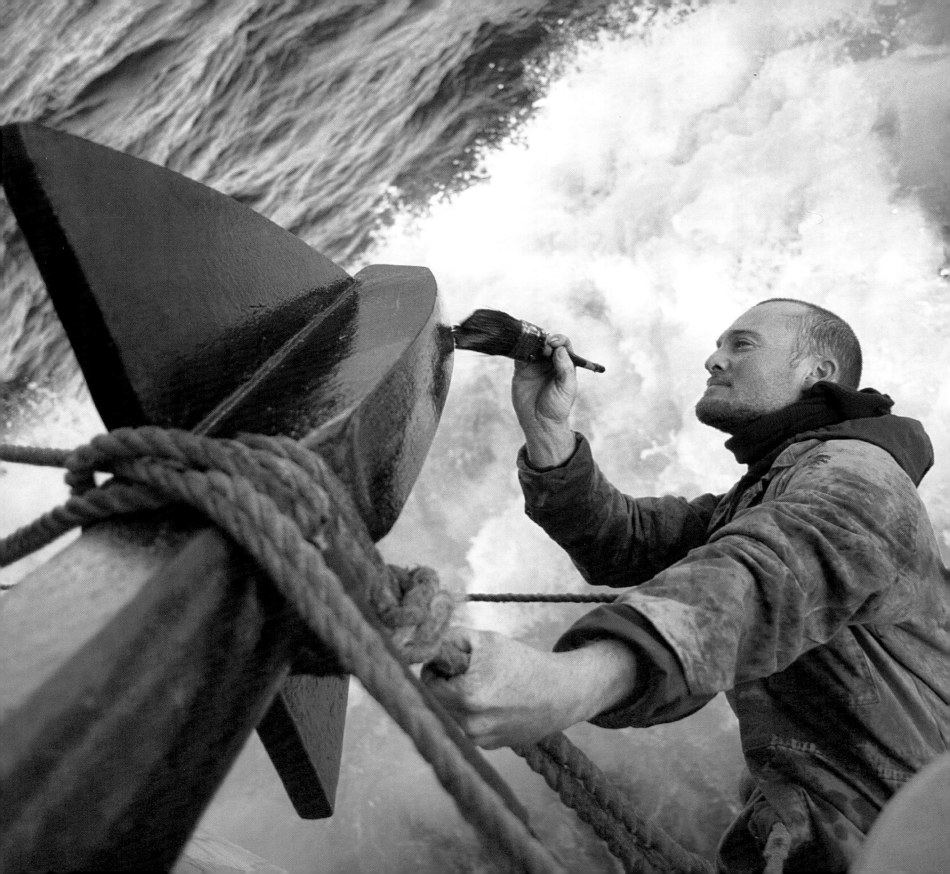

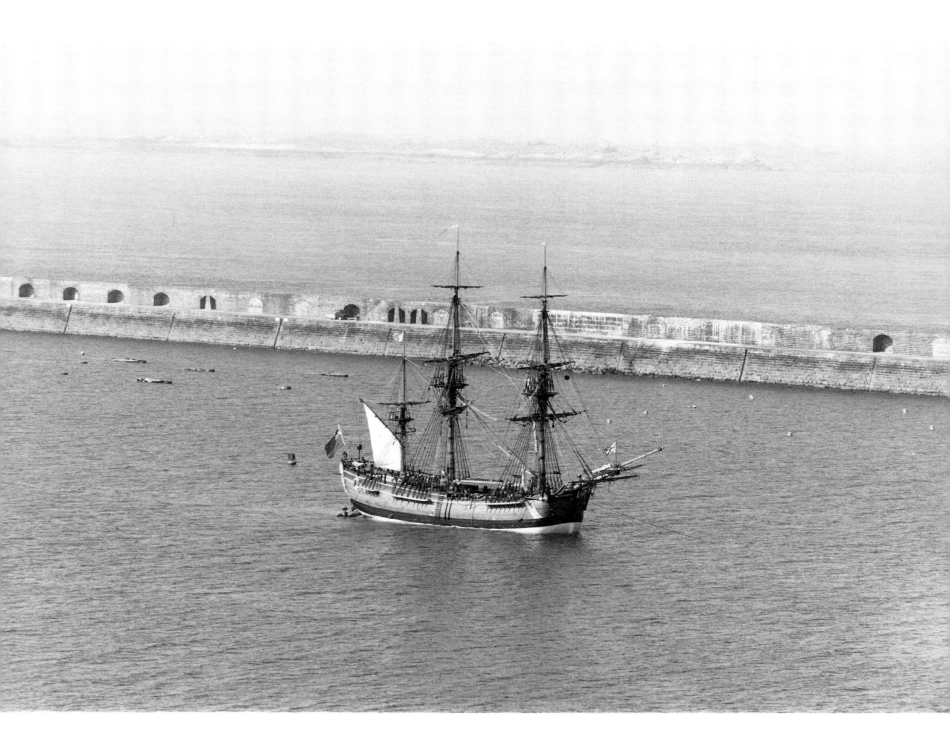

*Endeavour* at anchor, Alderney, Channel Islands.

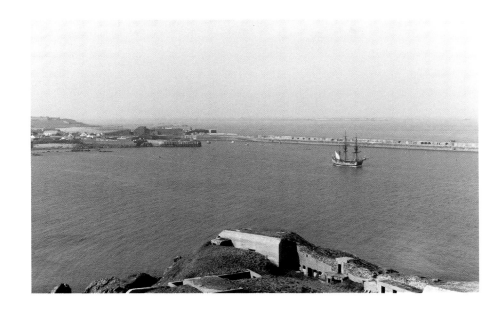

*Our course took us across the Bay of Biscay passing out of sight of Cape Finisterre and through the Passage du Fromveur. After rounding the Cape, Endeavour left the French coast, passed between the islands of Guernsey and Sark to come to anchor in Alderney.*

Captain Chris Blake, 1997.

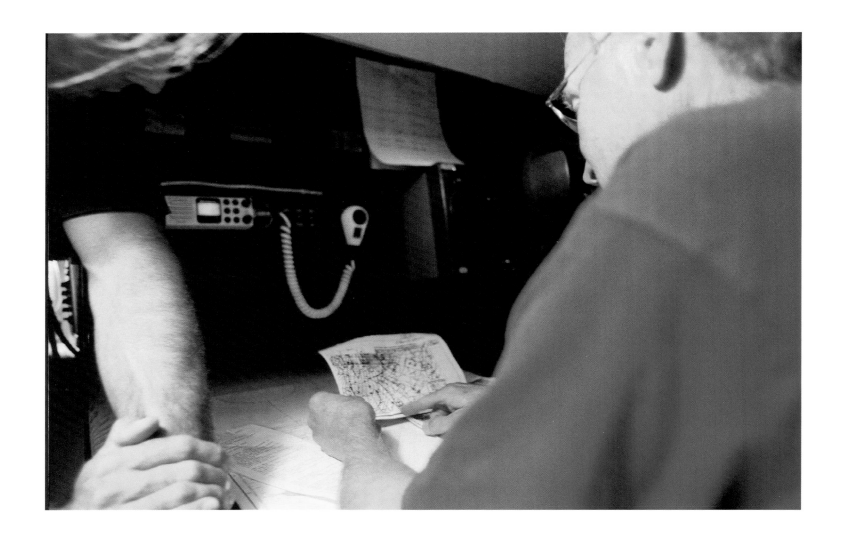

The Captain checks a weather fax.

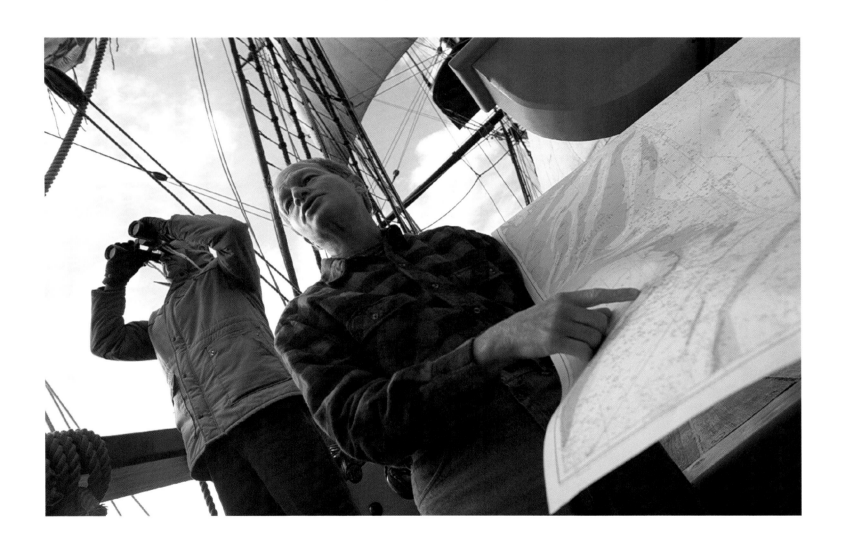

Captain Chris Blake briefs the crew as Clyde Ambrose keeps watch.

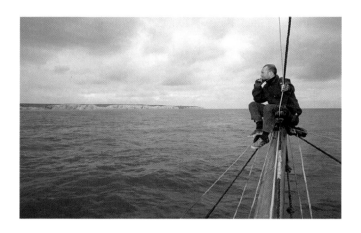

*Winds at SW a fresh gale with which we Run briskly up Channell. At half past 3 PM pass'd the Bill of Portland and at 7 Peverell point. At 6 AM pass'd Beachy head at the distance of 4 or 5 Miles, at 10 Dungenness at the distance of 2 Miles and at Noon we were abreast of Dover.*

Captain James Cook, 1771.

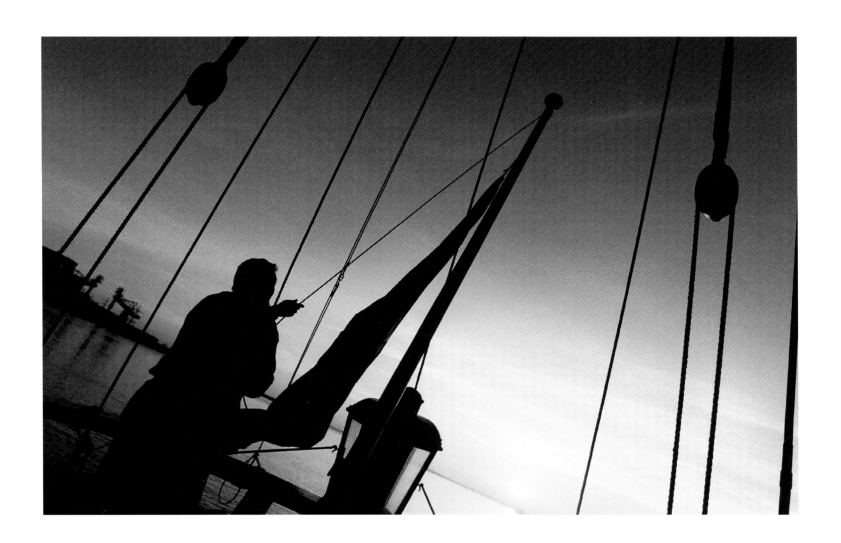

Striking the colours at sunset.

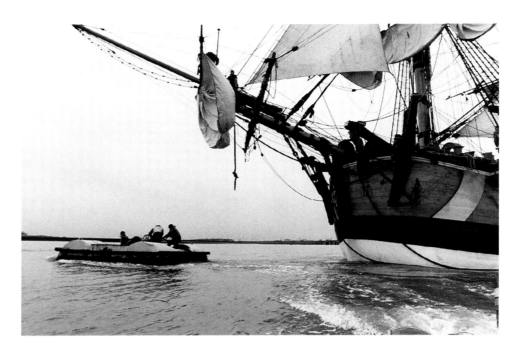

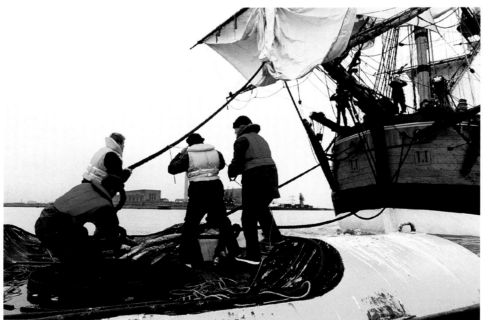

Mooring in the Thames.

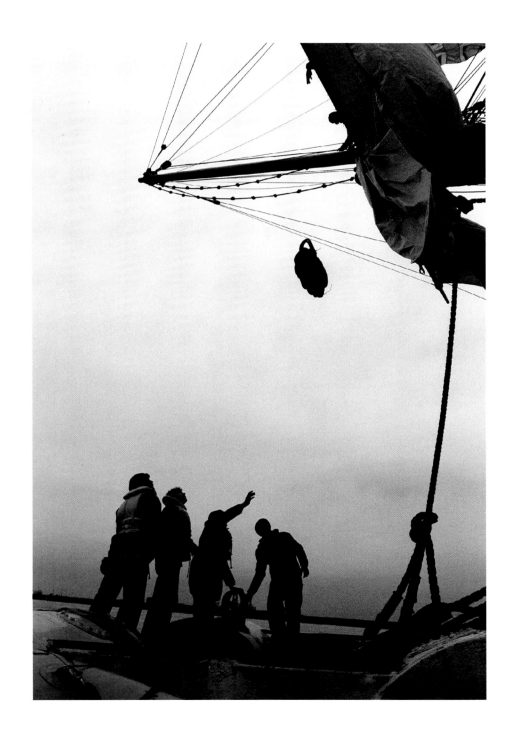

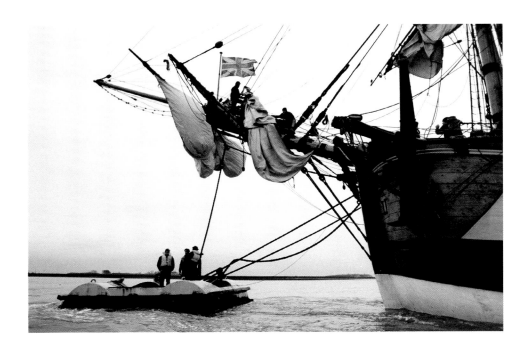

*We sailed through Dover Straits with a favourable tide entering into the Princess Channel of the Thames Estuary and anchoring half a mile off the Southend Pier. As we approached the more built up areas along the river banks, more and more people came out to see the ship sail past. Endeavour came to the mooring buoy at Gravesend at 1600, clearing all four cannon on picking up the buoy, much to the delight of the crew. Endeavour had arrived in London.*

Captain Chris Blake, 1997.

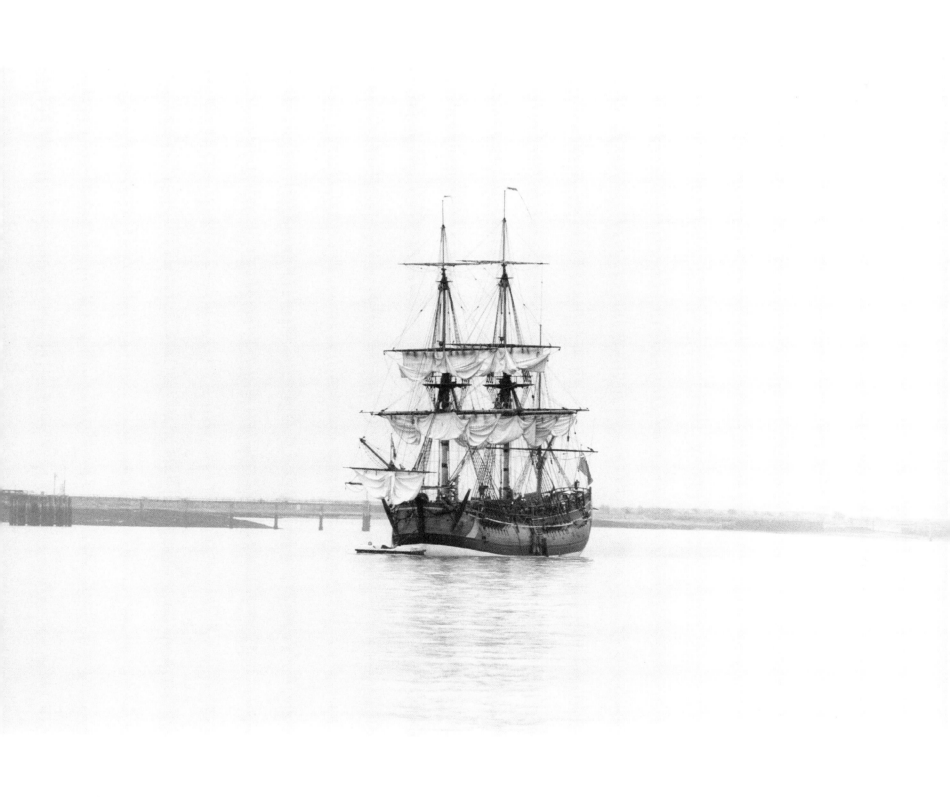

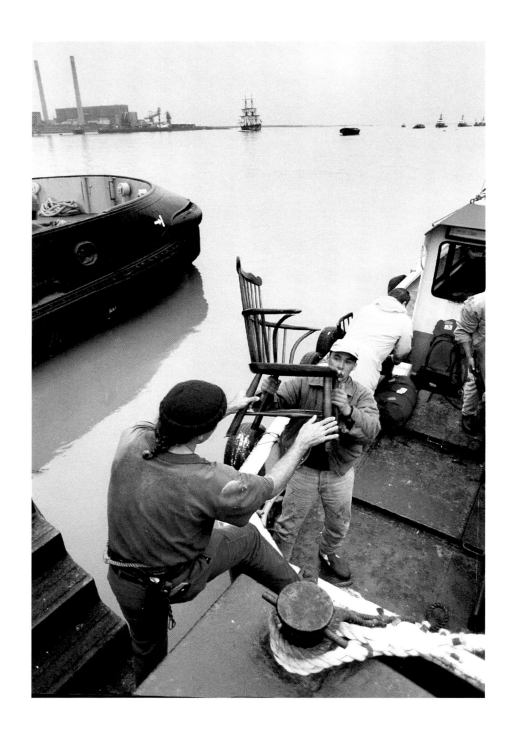

The Captain's chair comes ashore.

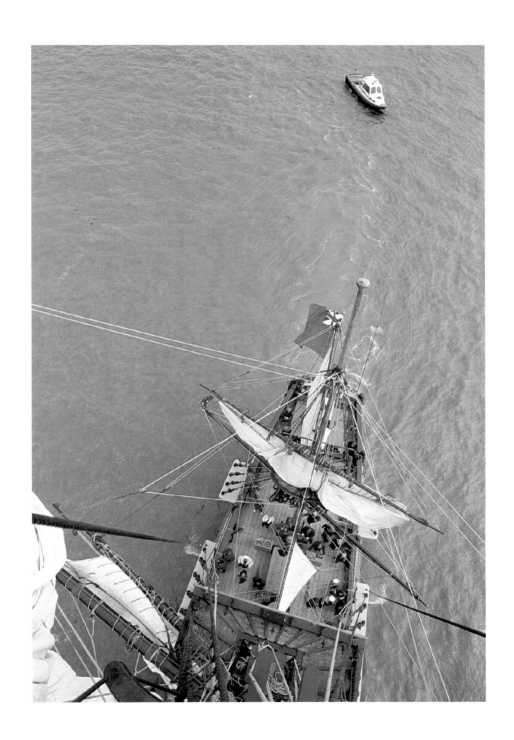

A pilot boat approaches *Endeavour*.

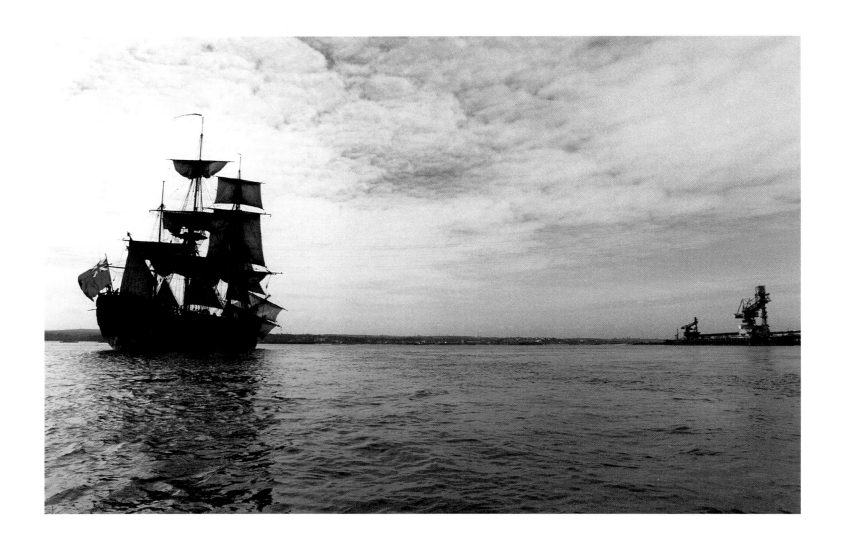

On the Thames.

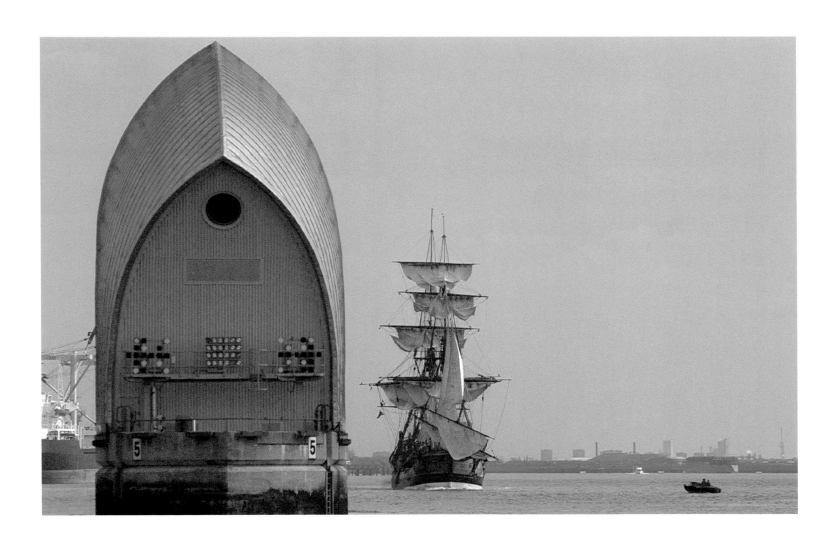

Sailing past the flood barriers.

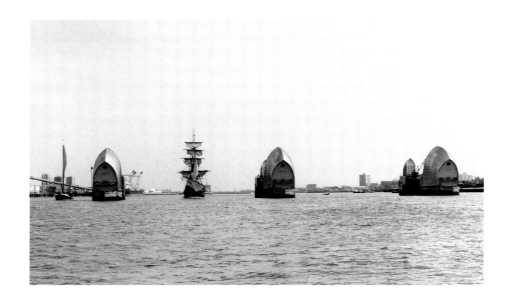

On the 24th Endeavour *was piloted up river to a swing mooring off Gravesend Pilot Station. The mooring was slipped on the morning of the 25th and* Endeavour *sailed up the Thames for her arrival at Tower Bridge.*

Captain Chris Blake, 1997.

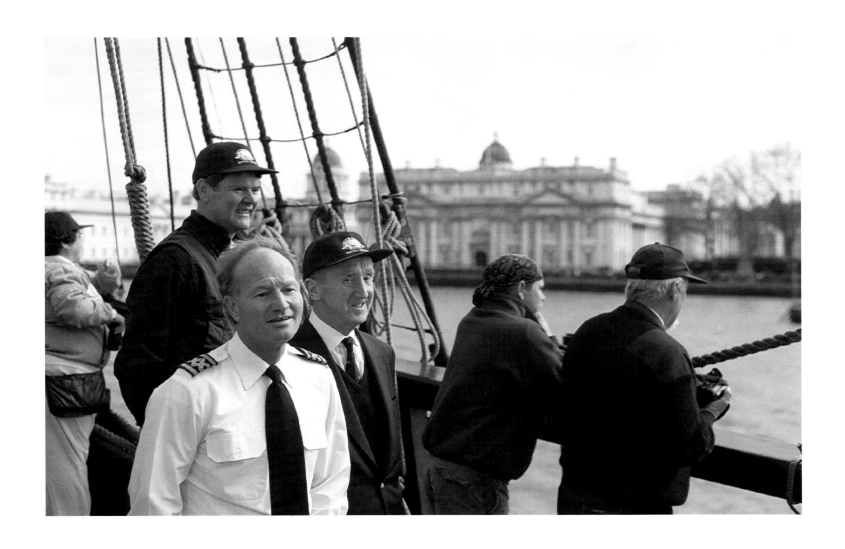

Captain Chris Blake, Chairman of the HM Bark Endeavour Foundation Sir Arthur Weller, CBE  and Foundation Chief Executive John Longley, AM (rear).

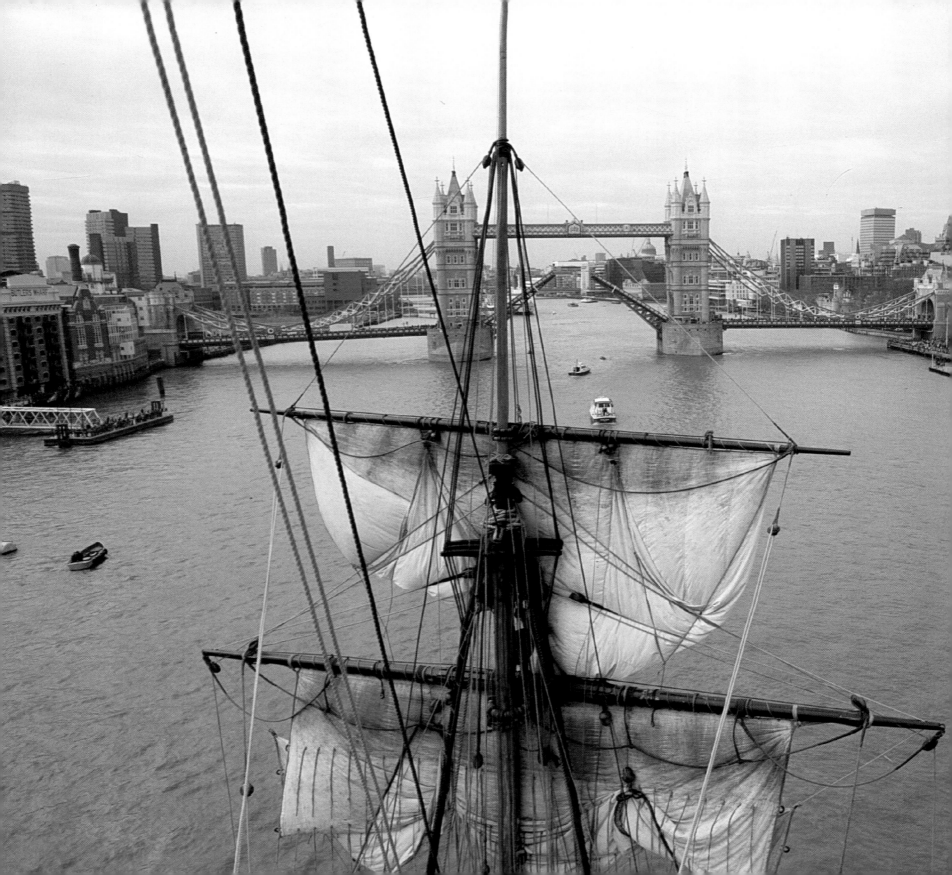

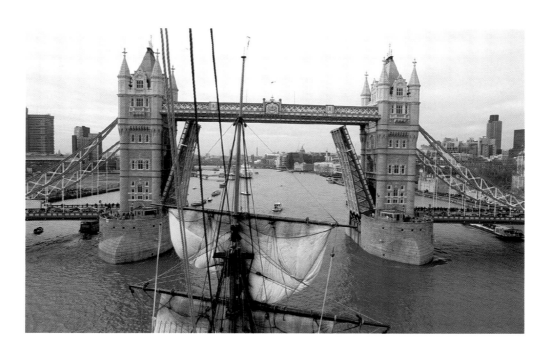

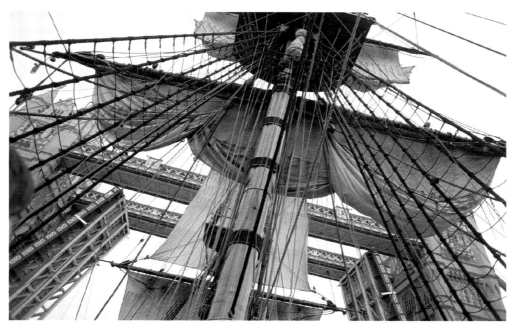

The Tower Bridge raises her road-decks to welcome *Endeavour*.

123

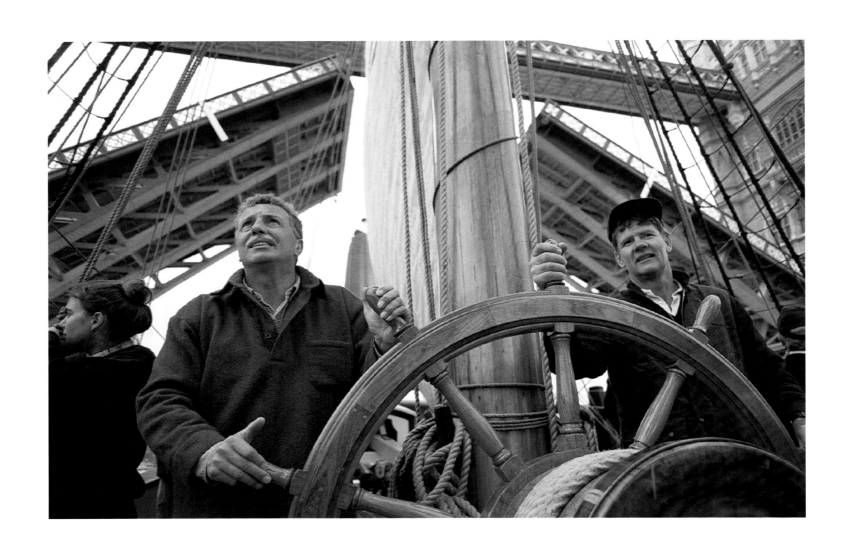

Gerald Collins and John Longley successfully negotiate Tower Bridge.

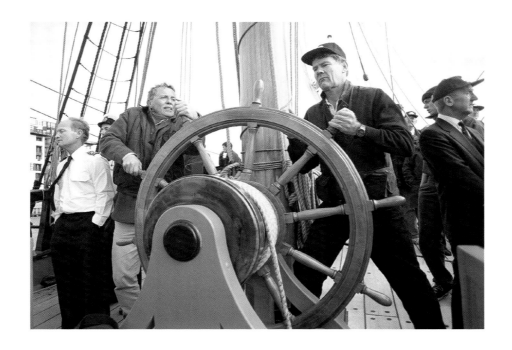

*At half past one on the afternoon of 25 March, Endeavour sailed under the Tower Bridge, London. This was an emotional moment for many on board, a great sense of achievement at this symbolic milestone.*

Calum Bennett, 1997.

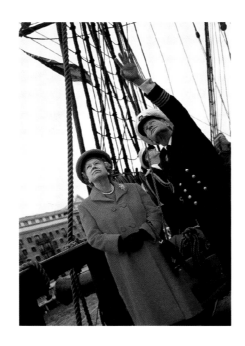

*Most of the crew managed a few words with Her Majesty the Queen and His Royal Highness the Duke of Edinburgh. Indeed our cook Joanna Mannington dropped all formalities and addressed her with 'Hi, how's it going?'*

Calum Bennett, 1997.

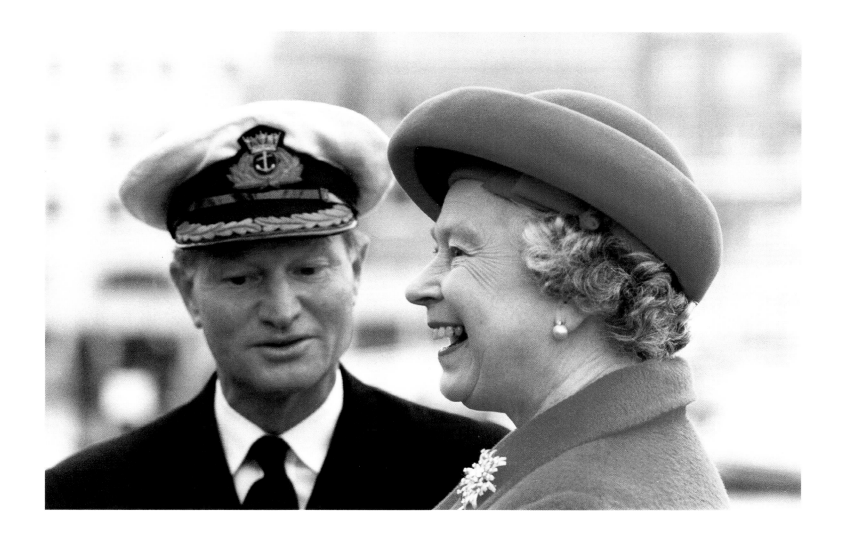

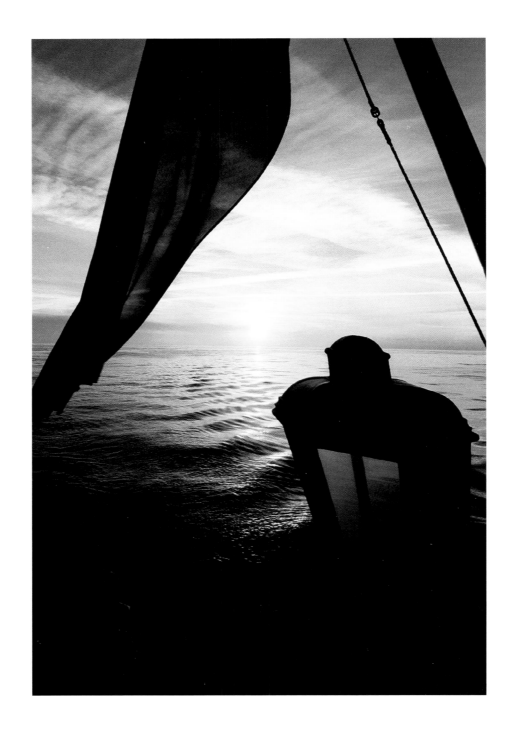

'All good things must come to an end' they say, and with a plethora of emotions ranging from sadness, euphoria, fear and excitement, we too must drop anchor on the voyage of a lifetime and move onto new seas.

But what a way to finish. Andy Warhol said we get fifteen minutes of fame – we had three solid days of it!!! The toast of London, we have been courted by the Lord Mayor, discussed beer with the Australian High Commissioner, chatted with Royalty and been cheered at and waved to by the throng along the Thames as we grandly paraded our ship.

Thus comes the final day. And we went out in style, friends that have shared a bevy of experiences that can only be summed up as 'We few, we lucky few.'

Now below decks there is darkness where there once was laughter and light. It is no longer our ship. But in our hearts those nights of dolphins and comets are still with us, and every sunrise will remind us of the beautiful light on the morning watches in the doldrums. I miss you already. We are different people now and our dreams have changed – ordinary lives will not be tolerated. May Neptune bring us all our desires and a life that is remarkable.

Craig Todd, 1997.

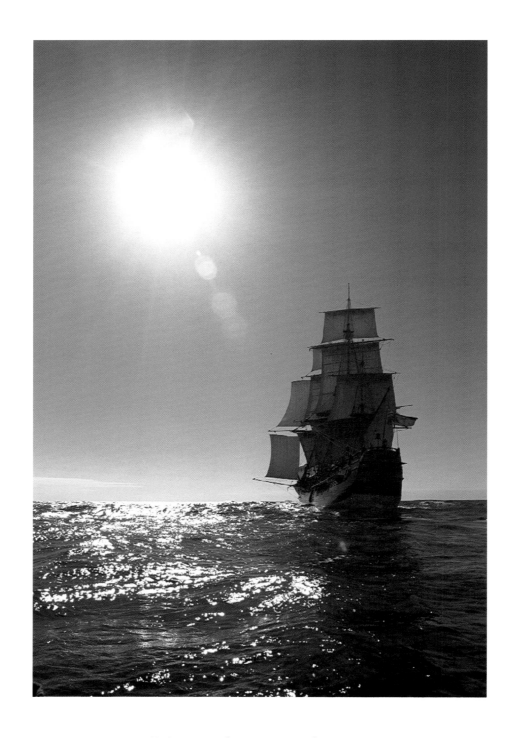

*Endeavour* sails on to new adventures.

# BACKGROUND

In 1768 Lieutenant James Cook, RN, set sail aboard HM Bark *Endeavour* on a voyage of exploration and scientific investigation. After observing the transit of Venus in the Pacific, he sailed south-west in search of the Great South Land. By 1770 Cook had reached New Zealand, which he circumnavigated and charted. Leaving New Zealand in March, Cook sighted the south-east coast of Australia a few weeks later. He discovered and named Botany Bay, explored and mapped the coast northward, and finally, on Possession Island in Torres Strait, proclaimed the whole of the east coast for Great Britain. Cook returned to England after three years at sea.

The original *Endeavour* was a three-masted coal carrier. Such vessels were the 18th century equivalent of bulk carriers and were built very solidly with flat bottoms, large holds and thick hulls. She was a slow but sturdy vessel, easily converted to accommodate a scientific expedition.

In 1987 the Trustees of the Australian National Maritime Museum determined to build a full scale museum replica of HM Bark *Endeavour*. A specially designed shipyard was erected beside the Fishing Boat Harbour, Fremantle, and administrative, design and construction staff were recruited. A company of eighty volunteer guides was enlisted and trained to conduct the public through the shipyard during working hours, seven days a week.

Work began on the replica in January 1988 under Bond Corporation, which took on the project as a bicentennial gift to the Australian people. The keel was laid in October of that year. In June 1990 however, Bond Corporation announced that due to financial difficulties it could no longer support the project. Yoshiya Corporation of Japan offered to complete the ship, but in December 1990 they too withdrew from the project. A group of staff and the guides, working on a voluntary basis, kept the shipyard open to the public while alternative avenues of support were explored.

In August 1991 a charitable trust, HM Bark Endeavour Foundation, was established to complete construction, commission and operate the vessel. The Foundation received considerable support from the Commonwealth Government, the New South Wales State Government, the Weston family, John Singleton and the National Maritime Museum (Greenwich), and generous donations from both individuals and corporations.

The *Endeavour* was finally completed and successfully launched on 9 December 1993. The research and construction of the replica took twice as long as Cook's original voyage.

The primary concern in constructing the *Endeavour* replica was to achieve historical authenticity. During its service as a naval vessel the original ship was surveyed several times and detailed information about it survives at the National Maritime Museum in Greenwich. The replica was built to the same specifications as the original *Endeavour*, and to standards certified by the National Maritime Museum and the Australian National Maritime Museum. Where differences exist they are to meet modern safety standards and/or to ensure that the vessel will have as long a life afloat as possible.

The main differences between the original and the replica are in the timber and the metal fittings used, and in the use of man-made materials for masts, ropes and sails. Instead of the traditional elm, oak or spruce, the replica was built mainly from jarrah, a native Western Australian hardwood. Old growth oregon, imported from the United States, was used for the masts, spars, topsides and decks. To prevent rotting, and for crew comfort, the replica has better ventilation than the original ship, and both modern and traditional preservatives were used on the timbers. The larger masts and yards are of laminated oregon; iron fastenings are galvanised; the running rigging is polyester; the standing rigging is manilla and the sails are made of Duradon — a synthetic canvas which looks and handles like flax canvas.

Some technical concessions to the 20th century have been necessary such as auxiliary engines, generators, a desalination unit, modern bilge pumps, heads, showers and an electric galley. The replica also has a complete range of modern communications equipment, including HF and VHF radio, Inmarsat M phone and fax, weather fax, collision radar and a Global Positioning System.

On 16 October 1996 *Endeavour*, under the command of Captain Chris Blake, sailed from Fremantle on the first leg of her world voyage. She arrived in London on 25 March 1997.

# ENDEAVOUR
## Specifications

| | |
|---|---|
| Name: | ENDEAVOUR |
| Type: | Ship rigged Bark |
| Nation: | Australia |
| Owner: | H M Bark Endeavour Foundation |
| Homeport: | Sydney, Australia |
| Keel layed: | October 1988 |
| Launch: | 9 December 1993 |
| Commissioned: | 16 April 1994 |
| Dockyard: | Mews Road, Fremantle, Western Australia |
| Tons displaced: | 550 tonnes |
| Tons gross: | 397 tonnes |
| Tons net: | 197 tonnes |
| Hull material: | timber (jarrah below the waterline, oregon above) |
| Length over all: | 43.7m (end bowsprit to the end spankerboom) |
| Length hull: | 30.92m |
| Length between perpendiculars: | 33.53m |
| Breadth extreme (hull): | 9.5m |
| Depth in hold: | 3.35m |
| Depth moulded: | 6.39m |
| Draught: | 3.4m |
| Sail area (all included): | 1462m$^2$ (stunsails are 531m$^2$) |
| Total number of sails: | 25 |
| Height of mainmast above water: | 37m |
| Type of motor: | Caterpillar (2 x 3406B) |
| Horsepower: | 404 |
| Number of crew | |
|     Permanent: | 13 |
|     Amateur: | 39 |
|     Guests: | 4 |
| Figurehead: | None |
| Employment: | Sailing museum replica ship |

# CREW

**Professional crew**

Master
  Chris Blake
Mate
  Geoff Kerr
Engineer
  Wally Mounster
2nd Mate
  Scott Fell-Smith
Chef
  Joanna Mannington
Boatswain
  Slade Morgan
Shipwright
  Danny McDermott
Bosun's Mate
  Gavin Reid
Sailmaker
  Anthony Longhurst
Topman
  Matthew Grey
Topman
  Penny Griffin
Cook's Mate/Topman
  Domonic Hannelly
Cook's Mate
  Richard Warnett
Steward
  Caroline McDermott

**Voyage Crew**

Stephen Adams
Clare Ainsworth
Paul Bailey
Tim Beaglehole
Calum Bennett
Michael Bosse
Thomas Bowman
Allan Brooke
Reg Brooke
Anna Brownlie
Jeremy Channon
Helen Charlesworth
Lindsay Collins
John Colvin
Mathew Cram
Jo-Anne Crowley
Donnamarie Dickens
Paul Dreadon
Zoe Egan
Tony Fowler
Collin Graham
John Harcourt-Smith
Michael Harris
Adam Harvey
Dougal Herd
Mark Heyink
Christina Jackson
Kay Jaumees
David Johnson
Karl Johnston
Roger Leevers
Marita Morgan
Richard Muggleston
Alison O'Neill

Mark Parer
Rolf Pedersen
Roger Peterson
Richard Polden
Michael Quarry
Gabrielle Ray
Ben Raysmith
Ashley Reichstein
Tanya Robbins
Anna Rothwell
Douglas Shaw
Dale Smith
Lyndall Thomas
Craig Todd
Ben Totty
David Turner
Todd Vidgen
Richard Warnett
Georgia Watt
Andrew Webb
Vivienne Wigg
Ben Willoughby
Debbie Wilson
Adam Wolfe
Barbara Young

**Supernumeraries**

Gerald Collins
Stephen Maycock
Desmond McLean

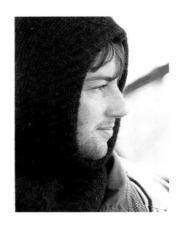

Richard Polden was born in Kelmscott, Western Australia, in 1971. He began work as a photographer with Community Newspapers in 1992 and moved to the Perth *Sunday Times* the following year.

Richard sailed with *Endeavour* twice as a news photographer before embarking in October 1996 as voyage crew/photographer on the first leg of her world voyage.

Photograph by Ashley Reichstein.